WEB Color EXPERT

A Friedman/Fairfax Book
Friedman/Fairfax Publishers
Please visit the website: *www.metrobooks.com*

This edition published by Friedman/Fairfax by
arrangement with The Ilex Press Limited
2003 Friedman/Fairfax Publishers
Copyright © 2003 The Ilex Press Limited

A CIP record for this book is available from the
Library of Congress

This book was conceived, designed, and produced
by The Ilex Press Limited, The Barn, College Farm,
1 West End, Whittlesford, Cambridge CB2 4LX England
Sales office: The Old Candlemakers, West Street,
Lewes, East Sussex BN7 2NZ England

Publisher: Alastair Campbell
Executive Publisher: Sophie Collins
Creative Director: Peter Bridgewater
Editorial Director: Steve Luck
Art Director: Tony Seddon
Editor: Stuart Andrews
Designer: Jane Lanaway
Development Art Director: Graham Davis
Technical Art Editor: Nicholas Rowland

1-58663-965-X

Distributed by Sterling Publishing Company, Inc.
387 Park Avenue South
New York, NY 10016

Distributed in Canada by
Sterling Publishing
Canadian Manda Group
One Atlantic Avenue, Suite 105
Toronto, Ontario, Canada M6K 3E7

For up-to-date links and resources, please visit:
www.webexpertseries.com/color

WEB Color EXPERT

ALL THAT YOU NEED TO CREATE YOUR
OWN FANTASTIC WEBSITES

KEITH MARTIN

FRIEDMAN/FAIRFAX

PUBLISHERS

CONTENTS

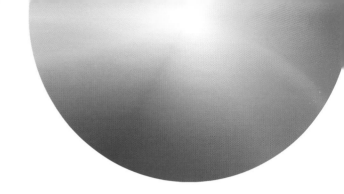

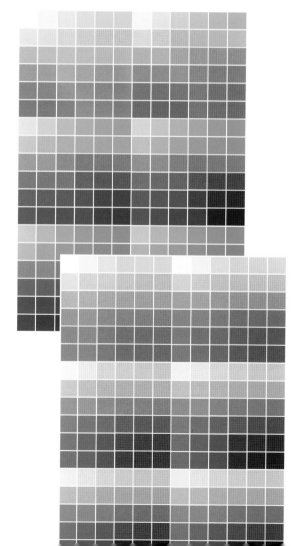

Introduction

Color is a vital part of any kind of design. From cars to magazines to clothes to logos, color helps to tells us what sort of thing an object is, as well as how important, serious, funny, interesting or otherwise it might be. This holds as true for that global publishing phenomenon, the Web, as it does for every other area of design. This book is all about getting to grips with color as a part of Web design, learning how to exploit it and how to deal with the difficulties that surround it.

Learning to use color in Web design—effectively and without technical hiccups—can be a challenge. The tools used to create the pages and the graphics that go in the pages can seem daunting, over-technical, and obtuse. That is where this book comes in. In these pages, we will tackle the problems of making effective use of color in every aspect of Web design, from the core constructions that make the pages themselves through to the graphics that flesh the designs out and—finally—to the rich, interactive, and dynamic media that can make Web page design so rewarding.

Web pages are still a relatively new form of publishing, and they bring new possibilities to the designer. There are many new things to learn, and many new issues to confront: the limits of screen resolution; designing for a flexible medium; the possibilities of multi-directional navigation systems. All the same, the fundamentals are no different from those in regular page design.

The significance of color

Color is something that affects us all more than we realize. It is precisely because we interpret color cues at an unconscious level that it can be such a powerful feature. Like a magician forcing a particular playing card on someone or ensuring their audience looks in a particular direction, color can be used to catch the viewer's attention, to bring emphasis to a feature, or even to direct visitors through a Web page layout in the right order.

Using Color

Color is not the magic solution to every Web design problem; it helps set up expectations and attracts attention, but you still have to come up with the right design ideas, and that takes practice. What's more, to really make your designs work you also need to make the programs you use work for you, and you can only do that if you know what they are capable of. The projects in this book are designed to explain both the whys and the hows of exploiting color in Web design. We can't tell you how to come up with the perfect design every time, but we can make sure you know how to get the best from your tools and avoid the most frequently encountered pitfalls.

And that's not all. Along the way, we will also show you how, by combining the potential of color and Web technology, you can create simple, stunning effects that will help your Web page stand out from the masses. If you think that moving color backgrounds, Flash animation and QuickTime movies are beyond your technical know-how, this book is going to show you that they are not.

Don't worry if you don't have much design experience. If you have ever put pen to paper and thought about where to put pictures and words, you have already considered the basics of designing pages. Since you first got your hands on colored pencils and paint you have thought, at least a bit, about how colors do or don't go together. Even if you have never seriously thought about design before, don't be put off. Formal design training is always a great help when you are tackling a large project, but with some expert guidance and experimentation you can still turn out satisfying work.

Finally, remember to have fun. Web design is an exciting new medium, and one that should be open to everyone. New possibilities are being developed all the time, and discovering and sharing new tricks, tips, and ideas is part of the whole experience. Above all else, keep exploring, keep practising, and keep using color!

Color Theory

Color plays a big part in the way
people judge what they see.
Everywhere you look—from fashion to
books, food packaging to websites—
you see color used in one way or
another. Sometimes it is effective,
sometimes it is not. Where it is
not, this is usually because those
responsible don't understand the
subtle language of color.

Color communicates things more
efficiently than most people realize.
In the first instant of seeing something,
even before the imagery itself is fully
grasped, the color used in the design
has said something to the viewer.
Learning how to use this color
language in your work is a vital step.

10 THE LANGUAGE OF COLOR

We use evocative terms to describe color all the time. Some hues are seen as warm, others cool. We speak of angry reds, calming blues, shocking pinks, and so on. Of course, the colors are just colors—we assign emotive labels to things ourselves—but remembering this association of moods and colors can be a great help when choosing colors for a design. You will probably do this instinctively to an extent, but given the state of some Web page designs it seems that not everyone's instincts are equally good. Visitors form an impression about a website as soon as they see it, so make sure you set the right mood with a careful selection of tones.

But don't think that this "language of color" applies universally across the world. What is a restful color in one country or culture may be a vibrant, even jarring color in another. For example, a couple of years ago in Japan, Apple Computer found that the sales of its "tangerine"-colored iBook laptop were significantly higher than sales of the "blueberry" model. Conversely, in the West this bright orange model was considered to be loud and a touch garish.

A lot of this depends on cultural context. Black can be sombre (funerals) or sophisticated (the "little black dress"). Red can be shocking, warming, or cautioning. It all comes down to what other colors are included, what sort of imagery is used, and, of course, the situation in which these things are seen.

The combinations of different tints and colors also make a mockery of glib assumptions about color. Put a dark, slightly brownish green next to a strong red and many would describe it as an olive green—a color associated with food and drink. Put exactly the same color with some browns and blacks and it is much more likely to be labeled khaki, and associated with military concepts.

Look at color with an open mind; notice how different sets work or don't work together, and what sort of feelings they provoke. Soon you will be picking color schemes with confidence.

1 *Apple's first-generation iBooks shipped in blueberry and tangerine hues. Sales figures showed that different cultures had very different color preferences. The 'no color' graphite model was introduced later as a special edition design, showing that even the absence of color can be a statement.*

2–5 *What does green mean to you? Combine a certain green with browns and blacks and it takes on distinct military overtones through color juxtaposition. Put it with red instead and the result would be more at home in a martini cocktail or with Italian food.*

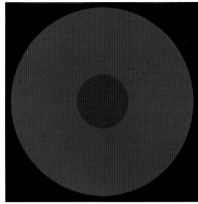

2

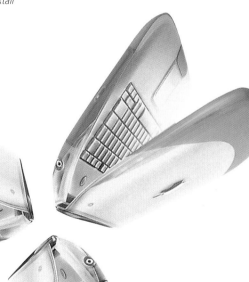

1

6 *It is the color of chilli peppers more than anything else that alerts most people to their spicy power; an excellent example of a cautionary red.*

7 *Pink is traditionally linked with particularly feminine concepts and very little else. This helps explain the impact of this photo of a combat-clad soldier in front of a pink cloud of smoke.*

8 *Yellow and black is the signature of the bee and wasp, and is used in warning signs around the world. But when found in the shape of a flower the effect is rather different.*

¹² HOW COLOR WORKS

Before diving into color considerations, take a quick look at how black, white, and grays work together. Place a gray square against a white background and it will feel relatively dark. Put the same gray square in a black background, however, and it will immediately feel much lighter. All tones are perceived relative to the tones that surround them.

The same principle applies to other hues; it just gets much more complex when different colors are compared. Place a mid-blue square on different backgrounds and it will appear bright or dark, calming or jarring, depending on what it is with. With a little knowledge of how the color you see actually works, this phenomena can be predicted, and even exploited in your designs.

To explain the ins and outs of this requires delving into a bit of color theory. This can be a very complex subject to tackle, and one that can take a whole book on its own. Fortunately, you don't have to understand the precise science and math that lies behind color, you just need a basic comprehension of how it is made.

1–2 *Which gray is darker? Even if you've already guessed that they're both the same, the one surrounded by white still feels darker, and stronger, than the one surrounded by black.*

3–7 *Take one blue and put it on different backgrounds. The perceived brightness and color strength is affected by the brightness of the surround, with the similar tones of the gray managing to subdue the blue the most. When placed with other colors the blue will either appear to blend in (if there are similar hues around it) or stand out (if the second color is complementary, with no trace of blue in its makeup).*

1

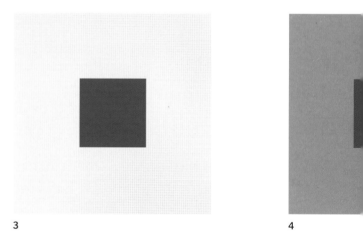

3 4

6

2

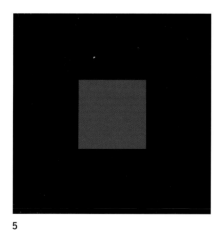

5

7

Additive and Subtractive Color

One of the first things to remember is that there is a fundamental difference between the color shown on screen and the color that you see on paper or any other printed surface.

Color shown on any kind of screen, whether computer or TV, is "additive"; it is produced by adding various strengths of red, green, and blue light together. Add red to blue and the result is a bright pink, lighter than the two colors on their own. Add green to that and the result is white—the combination of all three additive primary colors being the ingredients of white light.

On the other hand, printed color—or the color of any object for that matter—is "subtractive." The pigments or dyes in the ink absorb different colors from the light that shines on the surface, and what's reflected is the color that you see. Add red to blue with inks or paints and the result is a fairly dark purple. Add the third primary color, yellow, and—according to theory—you should get black. In reality, the result fails to absorb every wavelength of light, which leaves it a very dark brown. Still, the basic principle should be clear.

In print, the primary colors in print are red, yellow, and blue, although in commercial print the closely related magenta, yellow, and cyan are used instead. As a result, print-based designers will usually work with CMYK (Cyan, Magenta, Yellow, BlacK) in mind. However, it's different for Web design. Stick to the RGB primaries of light, as that is how colors are made on screen. When it is important to match printed colors, use whatever color mixing methods are available, but match things visually rather than using screen simulations of CMYK. As print designers know all too well, colors on the screen rarely match what finally appears on paper. In fact, there are some colors that can be produced only on screen: the restrictions of commercial four-color printing make it impossible to match the most vivid reds that monitors can achieve.

¹⁴ COLOR MODELS

If we want to make colors with the screen in mind, we can do so by working directly with the different RGB values. The problem is that working in this way is not particularly easy. Fortunately there are other ways to mix colors that are shown on screen. The method that feels more natural to most people is called HSB. This stands for Hue, Saturation, and Brightness (sometimes referred to as HSV color, with the V standing for "value," but it means the same thing.) Unlike mixing colors by changing RGB values, HSB color mixing involves picking the preferred hue (the pure color), choosing the saturation (whether the color is a tint or full-strength), and then selecting the brightness level. This last ranges from zero, which is black whatever the other settings, to 100%, which shows the full unshaded color chosen with the hue setting.

For a real-world paint analogy, think of the saturation control as mixing white pigment with a pure color to produce tints, and the brightness control as mixing in some black pigment to produce shades. Unlike the RGB method of mixing on-screen color, this is relatively simple to comprehend and manipulate, but the results are the same.

There are other color mixing methods on offer. The standard in Web design is the Web-safe color palette (see page 20 for details), but this is a fixed set of colors to pick from, rather than an actual mixing method. And while there is nothing to stop you using the hexadecimal code that defines Web-safe colors to create your own, typing codes is hardly the most intuitive way to work.

Every website design program also provides a way to use the operating system's own color mixing options. The standard Windows color picker offers a rectangular spectrum of color showing hue and saturation, with a luminance slider for controlling brightness. Luminance is like the brightness in HSB, but it ranges from black (no luminance at all) to white (full luminance). Pure untinted and unshaded color is achieved with luminance set to 50%—or rather "120," as the numbers go from 0 to 240. You just click and drag to pick a color, then alter the brightness with the luminance slider. The values for the color in HSL and RGB are shown as you go.

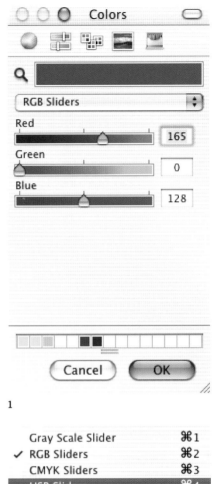

1

1 *The standard color picker in the Mac OS has a number of options, including sliders for mixing colors with great precision.*

2 *You can select your preferred color mixing mode according to your current needs, whether you're designing for print or for screen.*

3 *The color picker provided in all Macromedia products includes a standard Web-safe palette as well as ways to step over to the operating system's color picker.*

4 *The basic color picker in Windows is fairly limited, with the only real benefit being that it does help with consistency of color.*

2

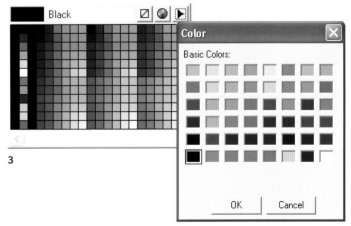

3

4

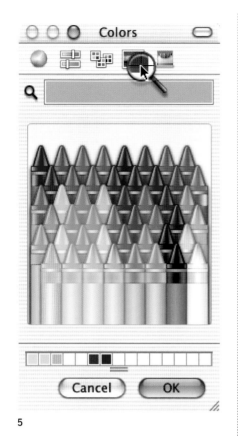

5

5 One of the more amusing color picker options in the Mac OS is the 'Crayons' display. More practical is the magnifying glass tool, which can sample precise color from anywhere on the screen.

6 The extended form of color picker in Windows offers a more flexible way to choose colors than the basic picker, plus, like the Mac OS picker, a place to store mixed colors.

7 Photoshop and Photoshop Elements use their own specialized color pickers by default. These have options for enforcing Web-safe color choices for those that need it.

The Macintosh system color picker offers rather more options. Some of these are more amusing than practical, but there certainly is a lot of choice. There is a similar rectangular spectrum to pick from, but there is also a classic RGB color wheel with a brightness slider; a useful set of sliders for grayscale, RGB, CMYK, and HSB color modes; a list of idiosyncratically named colors (from cantelope to nickel); and a set of crayons to click on. More importantly, there is a magnifying glass tool that lets color be sampled from anywhere on the screen. This tool is invaluable for Web designers, as it means colors can be picked directly from a scan, a page from a print layout program, someone's website, a video sample, or even a DVD playing in a totally separate window.

Both the Mac and Windows system color pickers have places for custom colors to be stored for later use. If you have just spent a while picking a precise shade, or you want easy access to a set of custom colors, add them to the custom color swatches list. The next time you use the system color picker, those colors will be waiting, ready to be clicked and used.

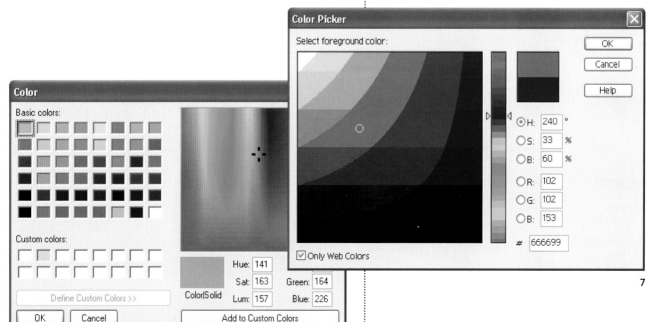

6

7

Practical Color

Now we have grasped the theory, it's time to get real. An understanding of perception and color models is important, but what counts is how that knowledge is put into real world use.

To get the best results, you should make sure that your set-up is up to scratch. There's no point in trying to color-matching decisions if your screen doesn't show you accurate results. But even that isn't worth much without a good, basic grounding in how color works in practice. Make sure you really know how your software works, how to choose the right set of colors for your work, and how your screen shows the colors you pick. Practical color is what this chapter is all about.

THE COLOR WHEEL

Color scientists have a lot to say about the relationships between print and screen primary colors, but when designing for the Web you should just focus on the practicalities of how to compare and mix the colors you want.

The most appropriate method of picking a color scheme uses the red-green-blue standard of the additive color system, as this is how the color on your screen is produced. Here, yellow is a product of red and green, a secondary color rather than a primary color itself. You can examine the full RGB color spectrum by using a color wheel, with the three primary colors—red, green, and blue—at equidistant points around the circle. Halfway between each primary color is a secondary color, made by mixing the adjacent primaries together. The secondaries are yellow (red and green mixed together), cyan (blue and green), and violet (from blue and red). Now come the colors that fit between each secondary color and one of the primaries. These are called tertiary colors, because they are a product of three colors; one primary and one two-part secondary.

Knowing the relationship between different colors can help when picking out colors for a scheme. A simple scheme can involve just one color, along with variants called tints (with reduced saturation) and shades (with reduced brightness). If two colors are used, you can opt for complementary (opposite) or related (adjacent) shades.

1 The RGB color wheel shows how the red, green and blue are spaced around the circle. Imagine it as a clock face; each primary color is four hours apart. The secondary colors are halfway between these, two hours over from each primary, and the tertiary colors are one each hour that is left over.

1

2

2 This design uses a few closely related colors with near-identical brightness levels. The result is a crude simulation of a Rothko painting, but also shows how similar tones and hues can merge together.

3

eq

the equus-equite lin

→ Horses and cavalry in Rome

→ Daily life as an equites Romani

→ Horses in the medieval era

Roman cavalry were ca Equites. They had to ov own horses, so the equ Romani (Roman cavalr generally well off. A few individuals who were p honored were given a h public expense, but mc were wealthy Roman c

home | search | archive | overvie

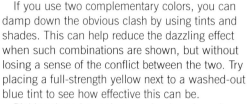

ver, by the third century
he ranks of the cavalry
being replaced by Gallic,
sh and Numidian cavalry.
se of this, the term equite
to be used to describe a
enatorial property-owning
rather than an actual
ber of the Roman army.

ch | media | bibliography | forum

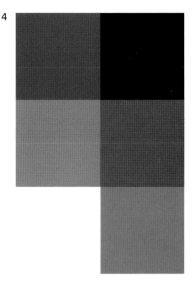

*3-4 Try picking a specific
and limited set of colors for
a page design. This uses a
simple set of six colors; black
and white, two grays, and
two red-based tones.*

*5 A site with strongly distinct
logical areas can benefit from
using different color schemes
for different sections. This
set of master pages sticks to
similar brightness levels—as
well as a distinct graphic
structure—but uses different
hues for each area.*

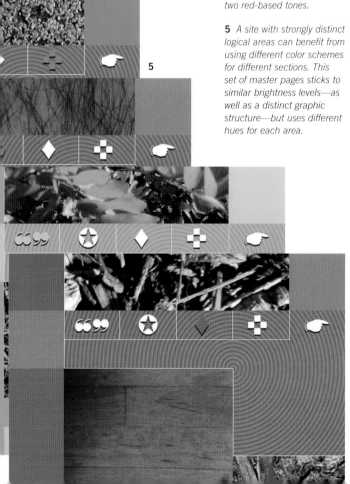

If you use two complementary colors, you can damp down the obvious clash by using tints and shades. This can help reduce the dazzling effect when such combinations are shown, but without losing a sense of the conflict between the two. Try placing a full-strength yellow next to a washed-out blue tint to see how effective this can be.

Picking three key colors can be done by using ones equally spaced around the wheel. Imagine an equilateral triangle dropped on top; pick the colors at each corner. This can be a very loud scheme unless a careful use of tints and shades is used. Alternatively, you may want to consider using just two of these three equidistant colors to reduce the visual volume.

For a much more refined set of colors, try using adjacent ones from the full primary-secondary-tertiary wheel. Unless you're trying to be particularly delicate, using just two neighboring colors is likely to be too weak. But if you pick three—for example the primary red and the two tertiary colors on either side—you have a subtle but usable palette, particularly with tints and shades on your side. Try using a darker shade of a color, with the brightness knocked right down, then moving around the color wheel a little for related tones. The results can be reminiscent of a less ragged Mark Rothko painting.

Many people have trouble remembering color consistency when designing websites, but keeping to a specific set of colors for key aspects of the pages is very important. You may have any color you like at your fingertips, but this doesn't mean you should use them all.

There are many ways of handling color consistency correctly, and most don't involve forcing your work into a "one size fits all" color grouping. For example, using different core colors for each page but sticking to the same method of tinting and visual layout structure means that pages can feel like part of a set without slavishly following the same color palette. Alternatively, using the same color in key areas across a site gives a consistent identity. This can make different sections of a site feel like part of a whole even when other color aspects of the various pages don't link together.

20 COLOR ON THE WEB

Mixing colors from color wheels is a good way to establish sets of colors and tones for a design, but there's more to using color in Web pages than just that. The infamous "Web-safe color palette" is something everyone should learn about, even if it is not as essential as it was a few years ago.

The Web-safe palette is a set of colors that can be seen cleanly by those with limited ability color displays, or those who have their screens set to a limited color palette. This is based on 8-bit color, which offers 256 different colors in total. However, the number of colors that are guaranteed to be the same in standard 8-bit color on both Macs and PCs is just 216. That may sound like a lot, but when you consider this has to cover every single tint and shade of each color, you will soon see that this is actually quite limiting.

Screens that aren't set to be able to show other colors cleanly will present approximations of them instead, by "dithering" colors together from the ones it can show. So, for example, a particular green that is not Web-safe (not part of the 216 color palette) would be simulated by using the two nearest Web-safe colors. These would be used in a pointillist fashion—a pixel of one color and then a pixel of the other, over and over. This does help fake colors, but the result is much grainier than a flat, Web-safe color. It is also particularly hard on photographic content.

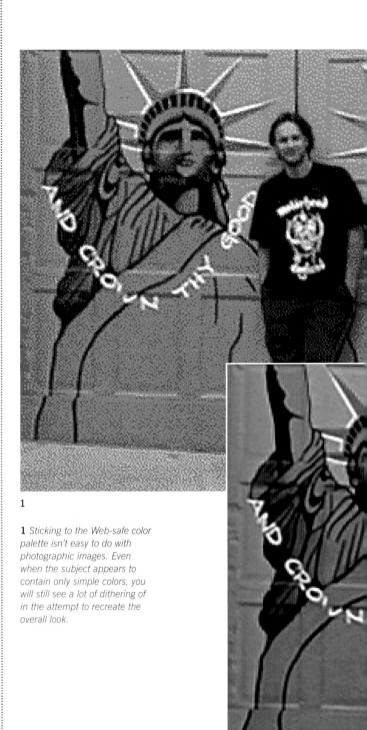

1

1 *Sticking to the Web-safe color palette isn't easy to do with photographic images. Even when the subject appears to contain only simple colors, you will still see a lot of dithering of in the attempt to recreate the overall look.*

2

2 *Using an adaptive color palette means using the most appropriate set of colors for the given image rather than sticking to a fixed set. The result will no longer be Web-safe, but it will look much better and the file size will still be small. This isn't always the best solution—this graphic would normally be better in JPEG format—but there are many different ways to use colors even when the total number is limited.*

Fortunately, today's Macs and PCs aren't limited to showing just 8-bit color. Modern graphics cards are perfectly capable of handling screens in 16-bit and 24-bit color, for roughly 64,000 and 16.8 million colors, respectively. These settings are also called Thousands and Millions on a Mac, and High Color or Medium, and True Color or Highest (also called 32-bit) on a PC. This means that virtually every computer has the ability to show a much broader range of hues.

But don't think this makes the Web color palette irrelevant. For one thing, a screen may be able to show millions of colors, but this does not mean that it is set to do so. Some games, for instance, will force a display into 8-bit mode but may not switch it back afterward. Many users rarely fiddle with any of their computer's settings, so things can be left in whatever state some unfriendly game set them for weeks at a time.

On a less gloomy note, the Web palette provides a useful standardized way to pick precise colors, whichever graphics or website program you are in and whatever computer you use. If you are asked to use a particular color in a design, it does not help to be told it is a "slightly purple-tinged red." If, however, you are told that the HTML hexadecimal color code you need to use is "CC0033" you can get straight to work in any graphics or site design program straight away.

If you need to match colors precisely without restricting yourself to the Web-safe list, feel free. As we explained, the majority of today's computers are technically capable of showing any color you care to choose. But do be aware that some Web-specific programs will try to be helpful by automatically re-mapping a color you carefully mix in the Windows or Mac system color picker to the nearest true Web-safe equivalent. There should be a simple option available for turning this behavior off or at least unlinking your hand-mixed color to the safe one, but don't assume that you will automatically be able to use a custom color without argument.

²² COLOR ON THE SCREEN

There are two distinct types of computer screen, and which one you use has a definite effect on the way you see graphics. First, there's the CRT (Cathode Ray Tube) monitor, the traditional bulky box built around a TV-like glass tube. This technology has had a long time to mature, and the screens are fairly inexpensive to produce.

The other type of screen is the LCD (liquid crystal display) flat-panel. Only 2.5–5 cm thick, it takes up much less desk space than a CRT, and is generally seen as more desirable despite costing significantly more for the equivalent display size.

There is, however, a definite drawback to LCD screens: they tend to have problems with color consistency. This is all to do with viewing angles. If you sit right in front of one of these screens, the image is fine, but should you change your position so that you are higher, lower, or off to one side, the screen appears lighter or darker than normal and

colors start to shift. If you move even further over, you may even see light and dark areas swap levels in an odd visual inversion effect. Obviously, this can make precise color matching and selection a bit of a nightmare. If you use an LCD screen, try shifting your position around to get a clear idea of how much movement is possible before things start looking wrong. You may find that your screen doesn't suffer from this problem much at all—some of the best LCD displays are virtually immune—but the majority do show it to an extent, and some are shockingly poor.

1 *Flat panel LCD screens are increasingly popular and affordable. While cheaper models can show different colors at different angles, with alarming results, the best screens are more consistent in their color fidelity. LCD production quality is being improved all the time.*

2 *The traditional CRT display takes up a lot more room, but there are no issues of viewing angle as there are with LCD screens. CRTs will be around for a good few years yet, but they are destined to be eclipsed by their slimmer cousins at some point in the future.*

1

2

CRT screens don't have the viewing angle problem of LCD technology, but they are still a varied bunch. The cheapest ones are generally the FST variety, a misleading acronym that stands for "flatter, squarer tube" but actually describes the most curvy kind of screen around. The worst examples resemble fishbowls and pick up reflections from just about everywhere. Displays that use Trinitron screens are generally much better; they curve in only one dimension, and generally not by much. You may notice one or two faint horizontal wires during use, but this unavoidable aspect of the technology is not usually too noticable. The newest thing in the CRT world is the "naturally flat" screen. This is literally flat, like a window or an LCD display, and is excellent for design work.

If you're worried by the possible color weaknesses of LCD screens—particularly the more affordable variety—but don't have unlimited desk space, look for the term "short yoke" when shopping for screens. This describes a newer type of CRT construction, commonly found in naturally flat units, where the "picture tube" used inside is shorter, so the monitor takes up less space on the desk.

If you already have an LCD screen but want the color-matching and consistency benefits of a CRT, you don't necessarily have to get rid of your existing monitor. The latest versions of Windows and any version of the Mac OS will happily drive more than one screen at once, although you may need an additional graphics card. Then you can add a second screen to your desk, placing some windows and palettes on one screen and some on the other. It can seem strange at first, but you will quickly get used to not having to hide, show and shuffle windows around when working on a Web page.

3 *Despite its age, CRT technology is still being developed. Short yoke tubes are making monitors smaller, and innovations are producing brighter, flatter screens that maintain consistent colors and geometry. With falling prices even large screens are now quite affordable.*

4 *Some high-end CRT monitors offer precise color calibration options and hoods for blocking out ambient light. These are really meant for serious print-based retouching and production work, although of course they are excellent for any kind of color work.*

3

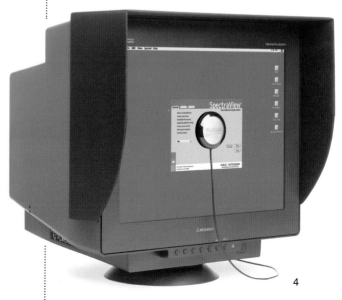

4

²⁴ COLOR CALIBRATION

For proper color work, you should seriously consider calibrating the screen to make sure it shows accurate hues and tones. Doing this properly can involve expensive specialist hardware, but you can do a little real world calibration yourself without spending a penny.

First of all, make sure the lighting conditions are normal. The room shouldn't be so dark that the screen is dazzling, or too glaringly bright. Now show a stepped grayscale ramp, which goes from 0% (white) through to 100% (black). Move the brightness control to around the three-quarters mark (a few monitors may need this set much lower), then adjust the contrast control so you see the lightest gray as slightly darker than white and the darkest gray as not quite as dense as the black. You may need to push the brightness up to manage this, but don't start with it at maximum. Once you have the brightness and contrast set correctly, see if there are any color controls on offer. Some monitors have them, some don't.

Try not to get involved in manually tweaking the strengths of the separate red, green, and blue signals, as it can be hard to know which settings to adjust and how far to go. Instead, look for some form of color temperature control. This changes the visual "warmth" of the display, helping to match it to the the ambient lighting conditions.

If the room is lit by regular tungsten lightbulbs then the light around you is actually a little biased toward red. Your eyes adjust to this, but the whites of things like paper will be comparatively warm and orange. If your screen is set to a higher color temperature, the whites on the display will look cold and blue. When working on images, it is tempting to compensating for this by adding warmth, but what you actually end up with is over-red results.

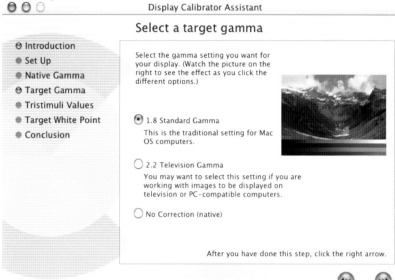

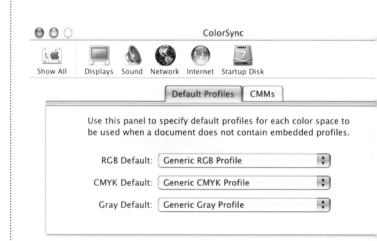

2

1 *Apple's Display Calibrator Assistant software comes as standard with the Mac OS, and helps users correct and switch gamma settings to get the best relative brightness levels on their monitor.*

2 *ColorSync is an Apple technology, but it uses industry-standard ICC profiles. The idea is to know the strengths and weaknesses of the relevant input, display and output devices in order to keep things in check. It isn't, however, really a calibration tool itself.*

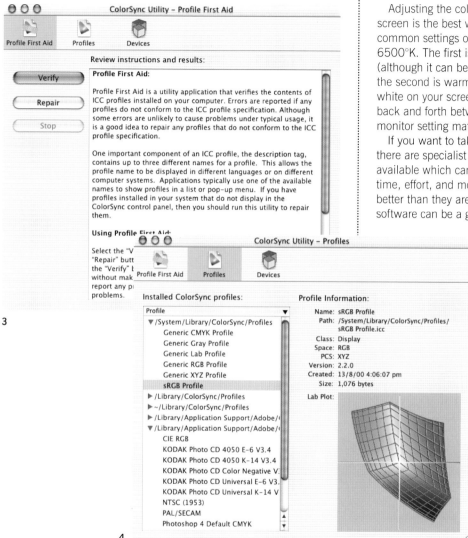

Adjusting the color temperature setting of your screen is the best way around this. The two most common settings on offer will be 9300°K and 6500°K. The first is fairly close to indirect sunlight (although it can be a little over-blue and cool), while the second is warmer and redder. Compare the white on your screen to some white paper, looking back and forth between the two, and see which monitor setting matches it the best.

If you want to take color calibration further, there are specialist hardware and software products available which can help, but be prepared to spend time, effort, and money getting things just a little better than they are now. Apple's free ColorSync software can be a great help for Macintosh users, although it really comes into its own only when applied from the beginning to the end of a workflow (scanning to display to output) and in every program involved.

Reasonably full but indirect natural light is the best kind of environment lighting for any kind of color work, and not just to avoid being dazzled by sunbeams. If bright sunlight falls on an LCD panel, this will eventually bleach out the display, making it more and more pale. This condition wears off after a few minutes of subdued light, but you should keep the screen angled away from south-facing windows to prevent it from happening. Direct sunlight doesn't affect CRT displays in the same way, although it does make things hard to see while the light is actually shining on the display. However, this kind of screen can actually become permanently and irreparably washed out if it is exposed to direct bright sunlight for months on end.

3 *The ColorSync utility provides a number of features for profile management. The First Aid section inspects the installed ICC profiles to make sure they are up to scratch. Problem profiles can be repaired to ensure consistent color throughout the workflow.*

4 *Other ColorSync sections provide an almost bewildering amount of detail about the profiled devices and their color space. The sheer quantity of information might seem like overkill to the average user, but it can make all the difference in a color-critical environment.*

GAMMA

One aspect every Web designer needs to remember when creating images for use on Web pages is the relative difference between the way images look on PC screens and on Mac screens. This is due to something called "display gamma," technically the effect that the input voltage of the monitor has on the intensity of the signal. Without adequate correction, the midtones and shadows of anything shown on a display are rendered darker than they should be. This can obviously alter the general brightness of an image—midtones look more like shadows and shadows become impenetrable—but it also affects colors, as hues made from particular values of red, green, and blue can look very different from screen to screen depending on the gamma.

Macintosh computers have their displays automatically gamma-corrected to a certain extent, which means that images tend not to be noticeably darkened by the monitors. PCs, on the other hand, don't have the same level of gamma correction (if at all), so the midtones of images tend to darken a little by comparison when shown on those computers.

You won't see the issue when working on your own computer, as you'll balance images to suit the way you see things as a matter of course. If you're a Mac user, you should definitely consider this problem because more than 90% of visitors to your site are likely to be using a PC. If you use Windows, you should also take this into consideration. Even if just one in twenty visitors uses a Mac, that can still add up to a large number of people.

The simplest way to counter this is to habitually turn your display's brightness up a little (if you use a PC) or down a little (if you use a Mac) every now and then. However, this approach is more of a global change than a specific counter to the midtone and shadow issues that are the root of the problem.

A more precise solution is to use the gamma simulation feature in Photoshop (although not, unfortunately, in Photoshop Elements) to check out bitmap graphics as you make them, because this is where the problem most often arises. Go to the Proof Setup option in the View menu and pick Macintosh RGB or Windows RGB as appropriate. This adjusts the apparent display gamma for images

1–2 Adobe's own Gamma Wizard, provided with Photoshop and Photoshop Elements, walks the user through picking the right gamma setting for thir display. The process is very simple, and helps ensure that the user's monitor settings are at least approximately correct. Every user should consider running through it every now and then.

3–4 The difference between the standard gamma of an unadjusted PC display and an unadjusted Mac display can seem minor, but it can lead to images being poorly optimized, washed out or a little muddy on the other computer platform. The first image shows the effects of a PC's common 2.2 gamma setting, while the second shows a Mac's default 1.8 gamma, which matches printed results more closely.

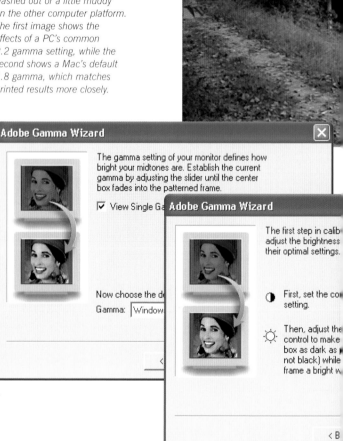

1

2

3

while you work, making it relatively simple to check for problems caused by gamma differences while working in that program.

Website design programs don't offer such features, however, so it can be hard to determine whether subtle tones in a Web page layout are going to turn to mud or wash out on other systems.

If you use a Mac, one answer is to use the shareware GammaToggleFKEY or GammaToggleX, from www.thankyouware.com, to switch your screen between different gamma settings at a keystroke. As this actually changes the display settings of the screen, it works with any program and across the whole display, not just a specific image. Another tool, for those that like to take more direct control of these things, is Gamma Control, from michelf.webhop.org/logiciels/. This utility provides a method for manually adjusting the gamma correction curve of a display, something that can be useful for general calibration issues as well as for simulating uncorrected or poorly corrected gamma.

4

28 COLOR-BLINDNESS

One issue that is usually forgotten when designing with color is the way things will appear to people with some form of color-blindness. This is more common than most realize. Around one in ten men, and perhaps one in two hundred women, have some form of color deficiency in their vision. This usually takes the form of red-green color-blindness, with the majority being insensitive to greens.

If your site relies on color cues for navigation elements, you may find that it is surprisingly difficult for some people to get around your pages. When the main thing that makes something stand out from its surroundings is its color, it could be effectively hidden to as many as one in every twelve visitors. Given the number of people in the world who have some form of color-blindness, it is important to know which colors are generally confused, and how you can avoid the problem without compromising your designs.

Color-blindness isn't a debilitating problem—most of the time, people with this condition have no problem with what they see—but those affected find that certain colors look almost identical to each other. A difference in saturation or brightness could be enough to help the color remain distinguishable; people that have forms of color-blindness usually develop a greater sensitivity to tonal changes. It's when the relative contrasts are too similar that separating colors becomes difficult.

1 *The impact a graphic has on a color-blind viewer may be rather different to what you expect. To avoid the worst of this, consider the relative tonal values of adjacent colors. If the pink here had been brighter in comparison to the dark background, it would have remained fairly easy to distinguish.*

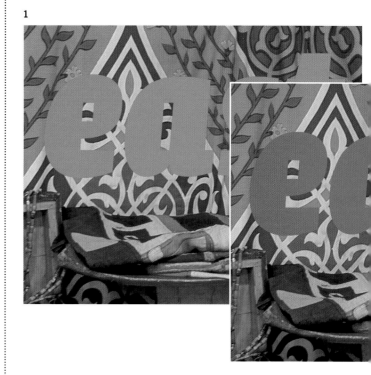

1

2

It can be hard just to look at a set of colors and know for certain which ones are likely to be misread and how, but there is software available to help. Mac and PC users can use ImageJ, a specialist image-processing tool found at rsb.info.nih.gov/ij, and add the Vischeck plug-in found at www.vischeck.com. PC users can also download a Photoshop plug-in from the Vischeck site. In both cases, the plug-in converts the colors in images to simulate the effects of a number of different forms of color-blindness.

As the Vischeck plug-in reveals, the set of colors in the Web-safe palette appears drastically different to deuteranope vision, the most common form of color-blindness. Pinks and violets turn to shades of blue, and the reds and greens turn to various forms of brown and yellow. This can have disastrous results for some color combinations, as the "east" example shows. The vivid pink letters are impossible to miss on the blue background for most people, but some viewers will actually find them hard to spot rather than hard to miss.

This doesn't mean you shouldn't use affected colors in your work. But you should remember that some combinations can be hard to tell apart, and avoid them where clarity is important.

3

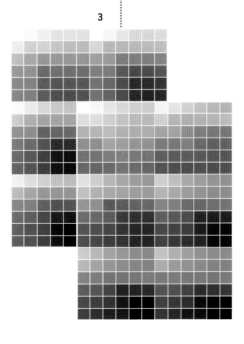

2 Considering the focus given by color can help produce better graphics and pages, regardless of color-blindness issues. These three designs all offer a measure of focus on the lower red dot, but the different uses of color in the rest of the image produce varying levels of focus on the dot itself.

3 Applying the color-blindness simulation software to screengrabs of the Web-safe color palette will give you a bit of a surprise. The result, with the most common forms of this condition, are a set of blues, yellows, browns and blacks. Reds and, to an extent, greens are absorbed into the rest.

³⁰ THE TOOLS

The programs used in this book are the ones found in most professional Web designers' toolkits. The key graphics packages are Adobe Photoshop 7 or Photoshop Elements 2, and Macromedia Fireworks MX. Older releases of these tools will often perform just as well, but some features are found only in the latest versions. Photoshop Elements is much less expensive than the full Photoshop package, and many users will never need the features that have been left out—layer masks, CMYK color support, and so on.

Other tools are required to create animated content. Most of these produce files in formats that require a Web browser plug-in to be used. The best known of these formats is Flash, and virtually every modern browser comes with a recent version of the Flash plug-in already installed. Flash exports work in the SWF (Shockwave Flash) format, and this has also become the standard output format for a number of other applications. These include Adobe Live Motion, a tool that creates Flash files but concentrates more on animation issues; Toon Boom Studio, which specializes in 2D cell-type animation, and Swift 3D, which creates 3D objects and animations.

The other key plug-in format that we will cover is QuickTime, the flexible and cross-platform industry standard for time-based media such as audio and video. For creating and editing movies, you'll need iMovie (bundled with current versions of the Mac OS operating system), Adobe Premier, or a similar package. Macromedia Flash can also export in a number of QuickTime formats, as can most other animation tools. Most of the tricks we reveal can be done with the $30 "pro-enabled" version of QuickTime, from www.apple.com/quicktime. The QuickTime VR work in Project 35 is done with The VR Worx from VR Toolbox (www.vrtoolbox.com), although other packages such as Apple's QuickTime VR Authoring Studio or Panoweaver from Easypano (www.easypano.com) are also perfectly suitable.

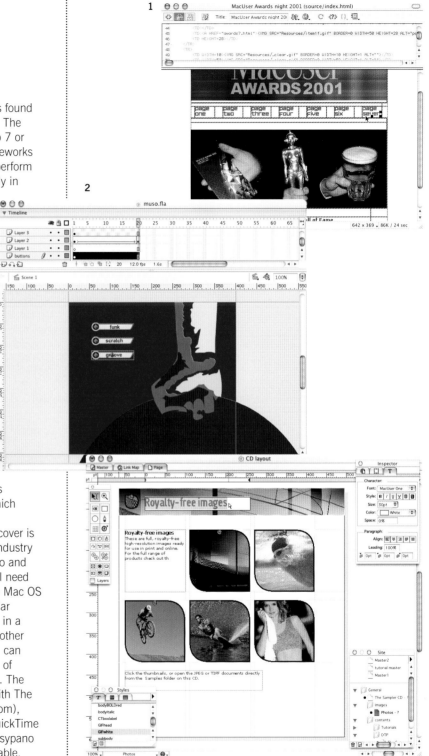

1

2

3

4

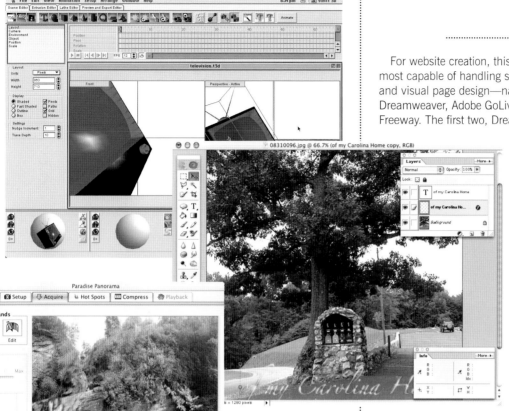

5

6

For website creation, this book refers to the tools most capable of handling serious professional tasks and visual page design—namely, Macromedia Dreamweaver, Adobe GoLive, and SoftPress Freeway. The first two, Dreamweaver and GoLive, are available in Macintosh and Windows versions, while Freeway is a Mac-only product. They are all capable of handling highly complex projects, but each has strengths and weaknesses not found in the others. The biggest difference between the three is in the fundamental way of working. GoLive and Dreamweaver edit HTML and adjust the underlying code as work goes on. Freeway is an HTML generator, so it produces optimized code from the designed layout on demand. All three let users customize the HTML code itself, although that sort of hand coding is not the focus of this book.

There are a number of other tools that users might consider adding to their collection. Mac users should download GifBuilder for assembling and editing animated GIFs; Graphic Converter for dealing with odd image file formats; Transmit for online file transfer (FTP) issues; and GammaToggle for showing the Mac and Windows color display differences. Windows users can take a look at Microsoft's free GIF animator or CoffeeCup GIF animator and CuteFTP or FTP Explorer, and they have their own version of Graphics Converter.

Links to the latest versions of all these tools can be found at the Web Expert: Color site (www.webexpertcolor.com) or at software update sites such as www.versiontracker.com. Plug-ins for checking color-blindness issues are at www.vischeck.com, and a cross-platform image-processing tool for using one of these plug-ins can be found at rsb.info.nih.gov/ij/.

1 *Macromedia Dreamweaver is the standard Web authoring application in many professional studios and has amassed a large selection of powerful features during its long lifespan.*

2 *Macromedia is behind the standard format for Web animation, and the application used to produce it: Flash.*

3 *Softpress Freeway has won favour on the Mac platform as the Web authoring tool that designers don't have to be afraid of, producing optimized code from any layout. Sadly, there is no Windows version.*

4 *Swift 3D can create complex 3D animations in the standard Flash format. It's also much more easier to get to grips with than the vast majority of 3D applications.*

5 *Adobe Photoshop is the leading image-editing package. The entry-level version, Photoshop Elements, is ideal for those working on a budget.*

6 *The VR Worx, from VR Toolbox, is one of several tools that can create Quicktime VR: interactive scenes, placed on a website that the viewer can "look around" in.*

CHAPTER 3

HTML Color

The bottom line in Web page design is the HyperText Markup Language, or HTML for short. It's the scaffolding that holds things in place, and the instructions that tell a Web browser to fill areas with color and style up text. In the old days we had to write the code by hand, but modern website design tools have changed all that.

You still need to know the principles of styling and coloring text, using tables as design elements, and so on, but don't worry—you will be able to get on with designing and coloring up pages without getting lost in the code. These projects start with the fundamentals of HTML color, then take you right through to some sophisticated tricks.

34 **PROJECT 1**
COLOR BASICS

Standing out from the Web crowd is what this book is all about. Develop a sense for using color on the Web—when to throw strong, jazzy hues about and when to tone things down—and understand how to achieve your Web design visions, and you will be streets ahead of most Web page designers.

This project tackles the most basic use of color in Web pages: setting up the color of the page itself, and applying color to regular text. This can be done easily in any Web design program—in fact, there's nothing more basic in Web page construction. Text formatting is the bedrock of all information design, and the restrictions that the Web imposes can present some very interesting challenges.

This project is not difficult, and it shows how things work in the three main Web design packages: Dreamweaver, GoLive, and Freeway. As it also leads on to the next two projects, there could not be a better place to start.

❶ **Dreamweaver** First of all, make a new page in your Web design program. We are using Dreamweaver for now, but the general principles are very similar in GoLive and Freeway. (We will take a brief look at those in a minute.) To alter the page's background color, go to the *Modify* menu and choose *Page Properties*. Click the color chip next to the *Background* label, and pick a dark blue, HTML color #003399, from the pop-up list.

❷ Click the *Apply* button to see the change without having to close the *Page Properties* window. The page background changes to your preferred color. However, if you put type onto this page, it would be black on dark blue, and hard to read.

To make your text appear in a different color, pick the right one from the *Text* pop-up color list.

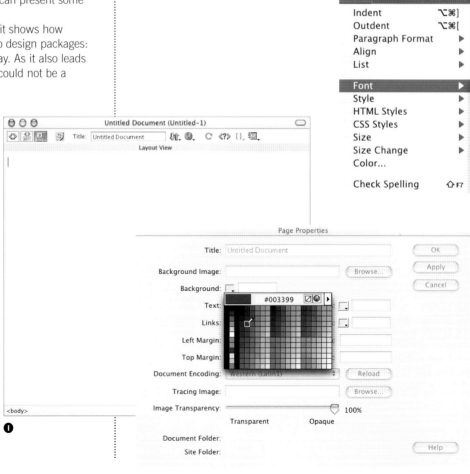

You can set any text color manually whenever you like, but using the *Text* pop-up is a sure way of getting an accurate color. Pick white, HTML color #FFFFFF, from the list.

❸ Now when text is typed onto the page, it appears white on the dark blue background. Select some of the text and pick the largest size from the *Text* menu, then pick the Verdana typeface set from the *Font* list in the *Type* menu. However, this isn't much better than working in a basic word processor; there's no appreciable control of where the text goes on the page.

❹ To get any real control over where things go in a Dreamweaver or GoLive Web page, you need to build a structure to hold things in place. The simplest way to do this is to build a set of boxes to hold the text where you want it to go. In the horizontal *Insert* toolbar, click the *Layout* tab and then the *Layout View* button, then click the small *Draw Layout Cell* button. Delete any text you have typed in already (this tool can't draw on top of things already in the window) and draw out a box in the left half of the document.

❺ Now type some text into this box. Note that it holds the characters in place, much like a text box in a desktop publishing package. You can click the edge of the box and resize it using the handles that appear on each side. Now draw out a second box to sit to the right of the one you have just created, and type some text into that one. Here we have formatted the text on the left to be as big as possible, bold, and aligned to the right, while the text on the right is set as size 4 and styled bold.

36

❻ Next, highlight the text on the left and pick *Color* from the *Text* menu. Use the color picker to choose a strong red: HTML color #FF0000 is as pure as you get. The large type is now red, not dazzlingly white, but it still has plenty of impact.

❼ Click in the text on the right, at the start of a paragraph. Now pick *Horizontal Rule* from the *Insert* menu. A horizontal rule will be inserted into the text, forcing the text after it onto a new line. In the *Properties* palette window, you can choose whether it is to have shading (for a simple 3D style) or not (for a flat bar). You can also pick its width and height—set the height to 5 pixels (just type 5 and press return) and turn off shading to get a thicker bar.

❽ The standard HTML rule is a kind of text object, and not very flexible. It is often better to use a *Layout Cell object* instead. These can be dragged around freely, although not stacked on other items, and can be given any fill color you like. Click the *Layout Cell* button, then draw a vertical box between the two text blocks. If you need more room, just enlarge the window to suit. Use the *Property* palette to pick a pale blue from the "Bg" color pop-up.

❾ **GoLive** Creating this layout is just as easy in Adobe GoLive. Make a new page, choose *Page properties* from the *Special* menu, and set the background color to #003399 using the *Web Color List* option. Drop a *Layout Grid* from the main palette into the page, then drag it out to increase the size and drop a *Layout Text* area onto the grid. Click on an item to adjust its size, and click inside the *Layout Text* area to type.

❻
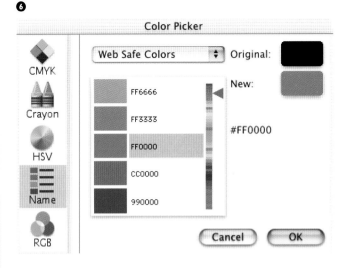

❼
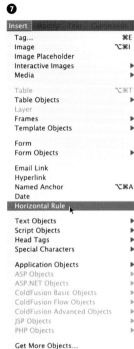

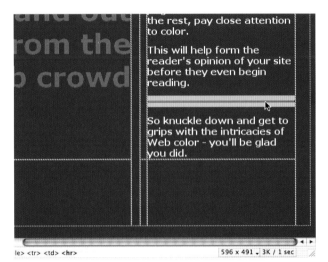

❽

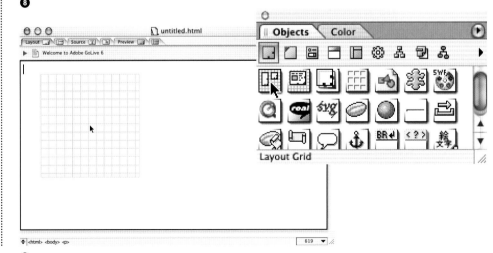

❾

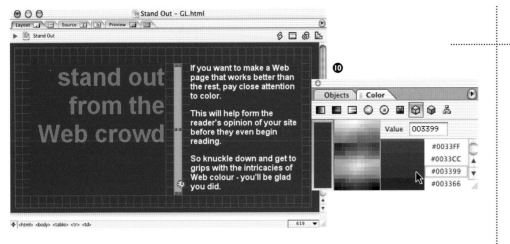

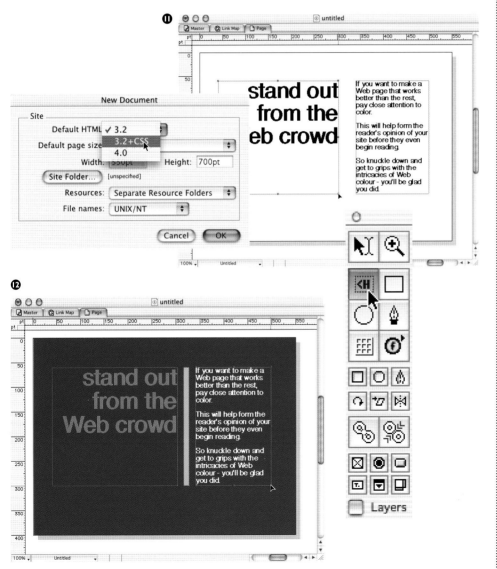

10 Use the Type menu to format your text. GoLive doesn't provide a Verdana font set in the Font list by default, so choose Arial instead (you can create your own font sets later on.) To set the text color, select it and click the small *Color* button in the toolbar above your page. Now you can use the *Color* palette to change text color. To change the color of a *Layout Text Area* box, select it and click the *Color* button in the *Inspector* palette, then choose your color.

11 Freeway To make this layout in Freeway, create a new document and set the *Default HTML* to 3.2+CSS. Begin by clicking on the HTML text box tool in the *Tools* palette and draw out the boxes on your page. You can click and drag the edges to adjust their size or position, and click inside to type text. Use the *Inspector* palette or the *Type* menu to format the text; pick Helvetica as the *Font* set and make it bold, then type 48 into the *Size* field to set the text to 48 point.

12 Setting colors in Freeway normally involves using one of the two *Colors* lists in the *Styles* palette. When nothing is selected, any change affects the page itself, otherwise changes affect the selected text or box. Click the fourth blue from the right, second row up, to set the page color, then select the text and click red for the left block and white for the right.

If you want basic HTML rules in text, select *Rule* from the *Insert* menu, and then edit the rule by clicking on the *Rule* tab in the *Inspector* palette. You can also make rule-type table boxes by drawing out empty text boxes to the desired height and width before filling them with the appropriate color.

38 PROJECT 2
BASIC DESIGN ELEMENTS

Designing pages involves far more than just pushing text around and giving it different colors. To move up to the next level, take charge of your page structure by using color blocks to mark out different areas. This can provide a strong structure to a page, defining sections and grouping elements together.

In the first project, we used tables to help hold text where we wanted on the page. This is possibly the single most important use of table structures, but we also touched on using them as design elements in their own right. Now we will push this further, using color to draw the eye strongly to the two sections of the page. Table structures can be used for color blocks and visual structures in their own right, not just as invisible scaffolding. Because of the restrictions of HTML, there are limits to what can be done, and if you are used to print-based desktop publishing, you might find these frustrating. However, with a little skill and creative thought, you will find all sorts of ways to strengthen your page designs without facing too much of a struggle.

❶ Dreamweaver Start with the Dreamweaver page we created in the previous project, and make sure that you are in layout view mode (see the *Layout* tab in the Toolbar). Then click on the right-hand text box and drag the edges in so that there is a space between it and the top, sides, and bottom of the *Layout Table* boundaries.

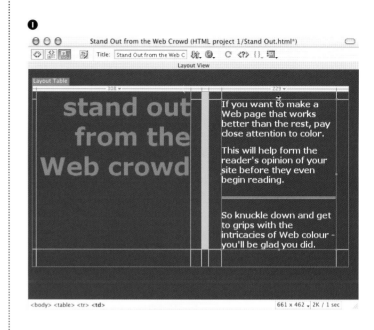

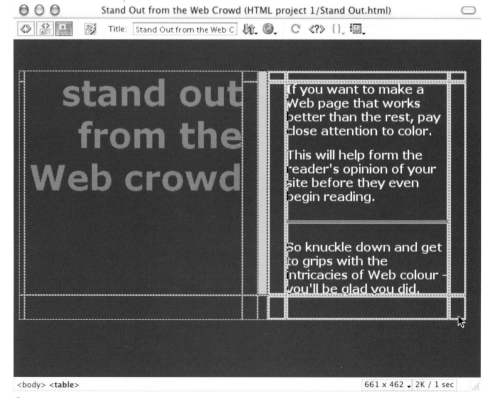

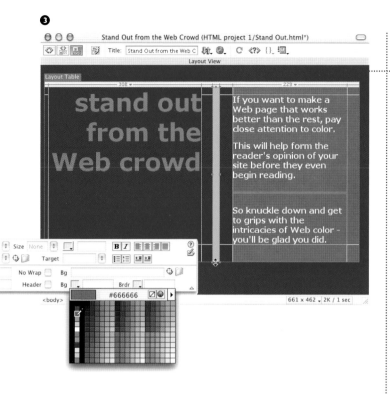

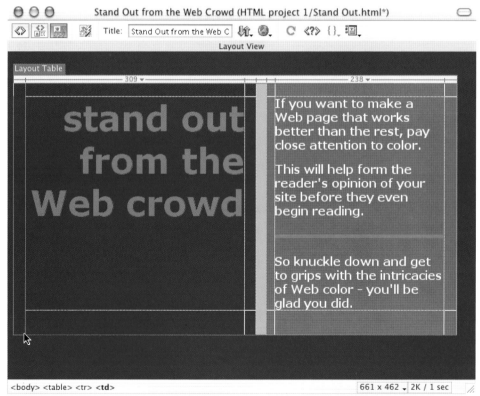

② Now switch to the standard view by clicking the button in the Toolbar. This shows your *Layout Table* and *Layout Cell* boxes as the regular HTML table structures that are used to make them. You can click in one of the blank boxes at one of the corners of the far-right text box, and drag-select over to the diagonally opposite corner. You should see the surrounding table cells become highlighted, as shown here.

③ Pick a mid or dark gray from the *Bg color* pop-up in the *Properties* palette; this turns the selected table cells that color. You can switch back to the layout view if you want to resize any of the boxes you made eariler, such as the vertical blue bar. Look out for empty table cells nearby losing their color as you do so—you will need to step back to the standard view and recolor them if this happens. You may prefer to stick to the standard view for now, as this "habit" becomes frustrating very quickly.

④ Before you leave layout view, however, resize the left text box to match the height of the right hand one and to give room on the left. Click the *Layout Cell* button and draw a layout cell into the whole vertical column on the right. Now click the *Autostretch* button in the *Property* palette. Dreamweaver asks how you want it to deal with this; just accept the default option of making a spacer GIF, save it to disk, and carry on. Draw a layout cell in the far-right column of cells as well, but don't make it autostretch.

5 You will probably need to step between the standard and layout views to tidy up any table structure oddities that have crept in here. Click into standard view to stretch and color cell borders, and use layout view to resize and color inserted layout cell objects. This can be annoying, but Dreamweaver's foibles are worth sticking with for the excellent results it can deliver.

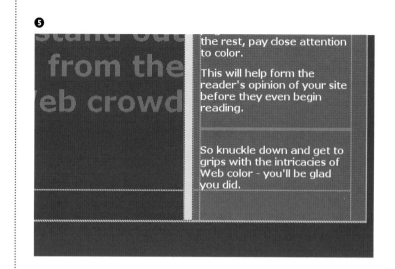

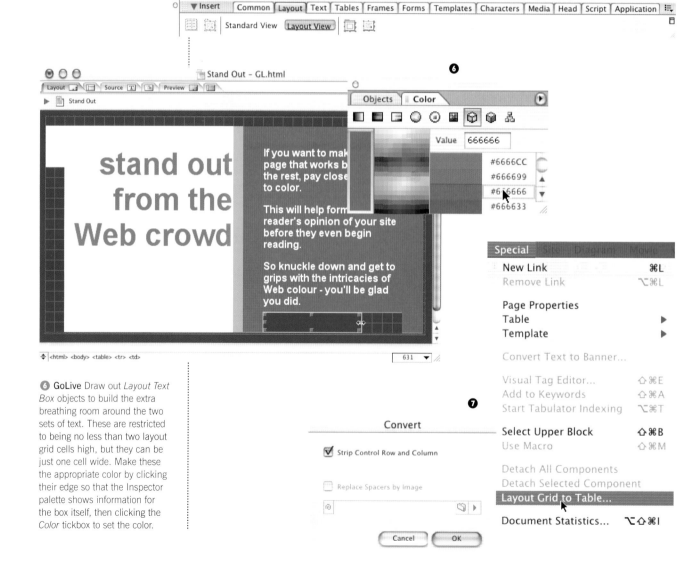

6 GoLive Draw out *Layout Text Box* objects to build the extra breathing room around the two sets of text. These are restricted to being no less than two layout grid cells high, but they can be just one cell wide. Make these the appropriate color by clicking their edge so that the Inspector palette shows information for the box itself, then clicking the *Color* tickbox to set the color.

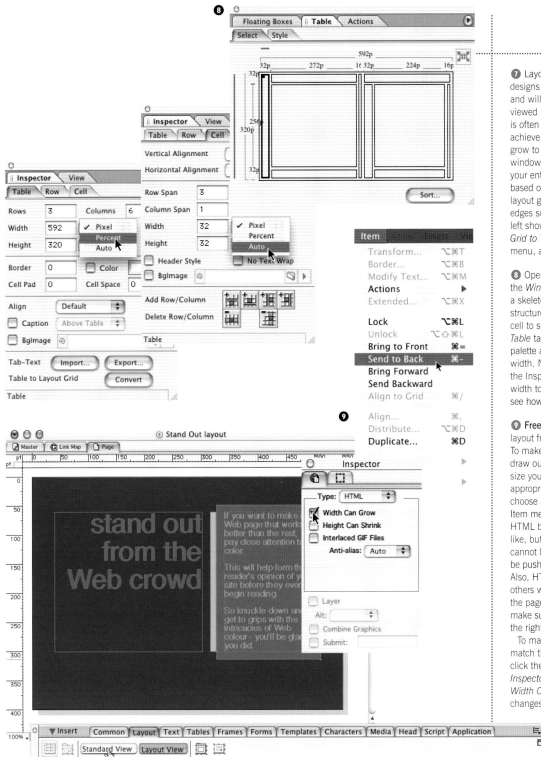

❼ Layout grid-based page designs are fixed-width items, and will not stretch when viewed in a Web browser. This is often what is wanted, but to achieve the trick of having boxes grow to fit wider browser windows, you have to convert your entire layout grid to a table-based one. Click the edge of the layout grid, and tighten up the edges so there is no bare grid left showing. Now pick *Layout Grid to Table* from the *Special* menu, and click the *OK* button.

❽ Open the *Table* palette from the *Window* menu; this shows a skeleton view of your table structure. Click on the left-most cell to select it, then click the *Table* tab in the *Inspector* palette and pick *Percent* for the width. Now click the Cell tab in the Inspector palette and set the width to *Auto*. Experiment to see how it affects your layout.

❾ **Freeway** Start with the layout from the previous project. To make the border effect, just draw out HTML boxes to the size you need, give them the appropriate color fill, and choose *Send To Back* from the Item menu. Feel free to overlap HTML boxes as much as you like, but do note that HTML text cannot be buried; it will always be pushed out from underneath. Also, HTML boxes on top of others will 'punch through' to the page color beneath, so make sure that you give them the right fill color.

To make the text box grow to match the browser window, click the first tab in the *Inspector* palette, then the *Width Can Grow* button. This changes the exported table cell's width from an absolute pixel size to a percentage. It will all work after publication.

PROJECT 3
COLOR LINK CONTROL

Without hyperlinks, the Web would be a collection
of disconnected pages, but merely adding links to
the text has an impact on color. In this project, we
will cover how to override the default colors used for
text links. Depending on your design, you may want
to pick appropriate colors that blend in with the rest
of the text or colors that stand out from the page.

The initial link color is not the only issue here.
We also need to deal with the Active and Visited
state colors if we want a coherent look and feel.
Active link colors are often glossed over, but with
a little consideration they can add another layer of
sophistication to a Web page's behavior from
lighting up the link to subtle dimming and the
classic disappearing "link blink" effect.

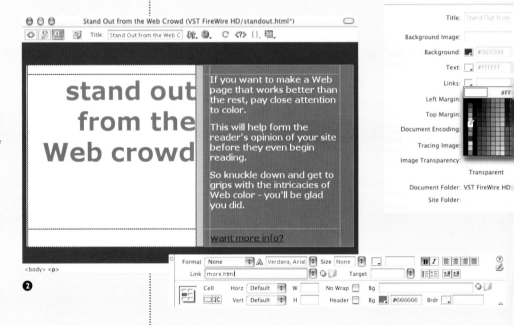

❶ Continuing with our
Dreamweaver example page,
type the text to be used as the
link below the right hand block
of text. You should have a small
separate cell structure below the
main one, which is perfect for
our needs. Select the text once
you have typed it, and format it
to match the text above; use the
Verdana font set, and bold. It
should already be white, as we
set this as the default text color
in the first project.

❷ Now the text must be given
a link address: a reference to
another page. We will use the
simplest kind of address—a
relative link to a page sitting in
the same folder—so we don't
have to include anything more
than the file's name. Type
"more.html" into the *Link* text
box in the *Property* palette,
and press the Return key.

By default, text used as links is colored blue. This is a leftover from when all Web text was black and all pages were gray; links were made blue to help users spot them. There are two other default colors associated with text links. As well as the link color itself, there's the "active" color and the "visited" color. The first is used when the link is actually being clicked on. The second replaces the link color when the page it links to has been visited recently.

❸ In this case, blue is not the best color for text. Go to the *Modify* menu and choose *Page Properties*. In the *Link* pop-up color picker, choose white from the set of swatches on the left. This sets all link text in this page to white. Add two more links to this page to give three separate lines of link text.

❹ The link text color now suits the page. However, when someone clicks the link, they get a brief flash of the active color—in most browsers, a bright red. When they come back to this page they will see the visited color, which is an unattractive purple. Changing this is done in just the same way as changing the link color itself. Open the *Page Properties* window, from the *Modify* menu, and pick custom colors from the *Active Link* and *Visited Link* color pop-ups.

For a subtle effect, pick a color for the active link that is the same as or very similar to the background color behind it. When someone clicks on the link, they will experience a brief "blink" effect as the item disappears for a split second. This is too short a time to cause problems, and the small visual change lets the user know that the link has been clicked without an excess of fanfare.

44

5 Setting the visited link color to be the same as the main link color makes sure that the user won't end up with a visual hodge-podge of shades messing up the appearance of the text on the page. However, while this can be useful for some pages, it doesn't help the user if there are many links; they can't tell which ones they have visited. To make life easier for someone using the page as a jumping-off point to many other places, set the visited link color to something other than the regular link color. Don't make the change too dramatic; a small change of hue can be just enough to show the reader that there is a difference.

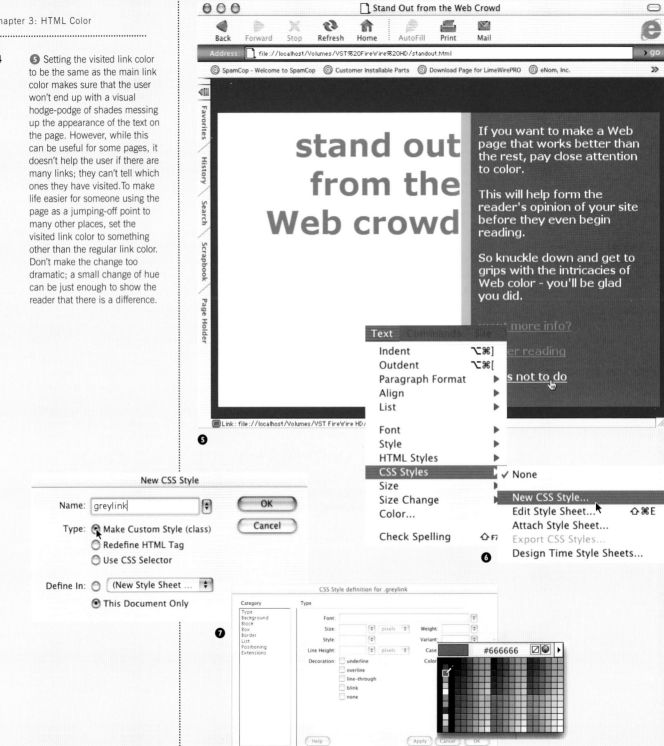

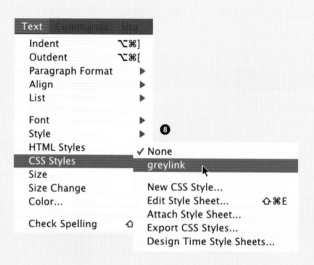

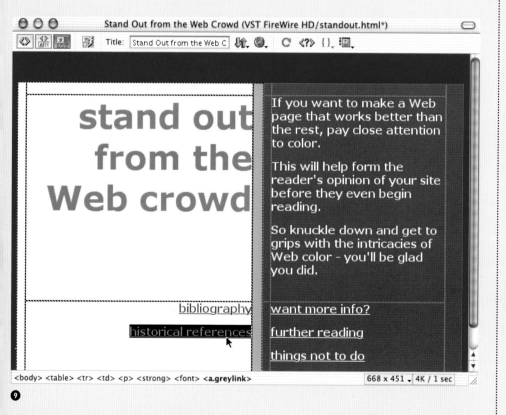

6 The trouble with white link text is that it is invisible when shown on a white background. If you want to have multiple link colors on a single page, you will need to set this up using CSS (Cascading Style Sheets). CSS extends the standard features of HTML to open up some more sophisticated methods of styling the objects on your page. By applying a CSS style to an object, you can override the page-wide color scheme. Go to *CSS Styles* in the *Text* menu and pick *New CSS Style*.

7 Name the new style "graylink", then pick a medium or dark gray from the pop-up color picker. This creates a CSS style that overrides the color of any text it formats, but will not alter any other settings.

8 Add some text in the left-hand white section of the page, then turn the text into links. They disappear as you do so, because they are shown as white on white. To fix this, select the text (double-click and drag over the invisible words), then go to *CSS Styles* in the *Text* menu and pick "graylink" from the submenu.

9 Now things are working as they should: the page-level white link color is working for plain linked text, and you are able to override that with your custom CSS-defined text color wherever necessary. Don't go oveboard. If you are too wild with setting multiple link colors, you will probably end up with a very confusing page indeed.

46 PROJECT 4
BACKGROUND COLOR PAGE TRANSITIONS

Page colors can be changed while a user looks at the page, not just when you are building the things in your Web design program. This involves using some JavaScript code, but don't worry: although JavaScript can be impenetrable to all but the most dedicated programmers, it's not hard to make use of small, self-contained chunks in your pages.

The triggers that cause this background color change to happen can be as subtle as a simple "onMouseOver" rollover or as obvious as a chunky form button that needs to be clicked.

What makes this technical trick worth remembering is the way that it can hide and reveal elements by simply matching the colors used for different blocks of text or graphics. The elements aren't really hidden, though they are as far as the end viewer is concerned, because they can't be seen any more. Use this to focus attention in different places, to hide answers to a question until the user wants to see them, or for anything else you can think of.

❶ Using Dreamweaver, make a new document. Use the *Insert* toolbar to step to *Layout View*, then draw a couple of layout boxes side by side. Type the same text as in project 1: "stand out from the Web crowd" and so on, into the two boxes, then draw out a couple of shorter boxes beneath and type "how?" and "what?" into them. Once you've applied the color to the text, you should end up with a layout that looks something like the one shown here.

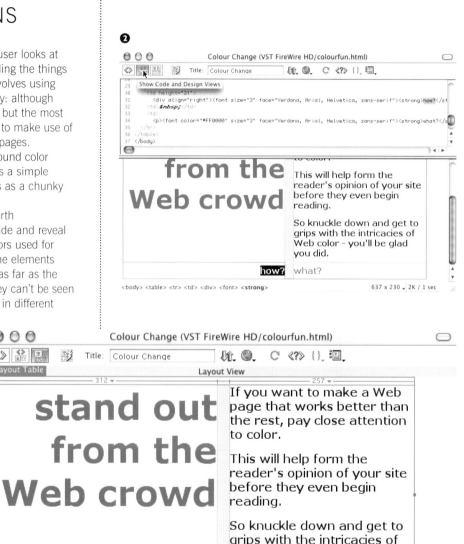

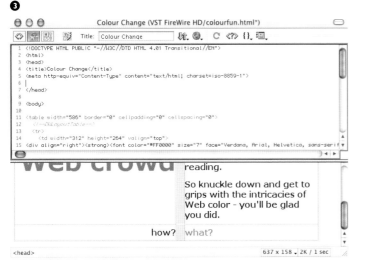

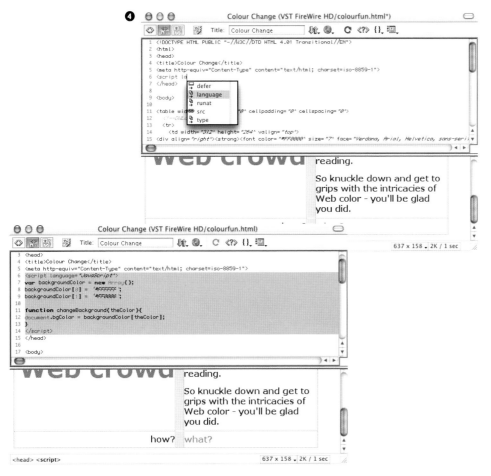

❷ Now we need to add a few lines of JavaScript instruction to the start of the HTML page. In the main document window, click the second button from the left at the top, or pick *Code and Design* from the *View* menu. Your document is split into two sections, with the layout at the bottom, and the HTML code that defines it above. Change something in either section and it will be updated in the other.

❸ Scroll to the top of the code view section, then click before the </head> text and add a new line. You may find it better to drag the dividing bar between the two sections down a little to give yourself more room.

❹ Now type the following text, being careful about spelling and use of the correct brackets, semi-colons, and so on. In particular, note where single and double quotes are used—these are not interchangable. As you go, Dreamweaver suggests portions of code that match what you're typing and adds matching "closing" portions of code where appropriate. When you are done, the result should look like the code shown.

```
<script
language="JavaScript">
var backgroundColor =
new Array();

backgroundColor[0] =
'#000000';

backgroundColor[1] =
'#FF0000';

function
changeBackground(theColor)
{

document.bgColor =
backgroundColor[theColor];
}

</script>
```

48

5 This code has built the background color changing ability into the page. Now you need to add the triggers that cause the change to happen. Select the "how?" text in the design view—you'll see it shown in the code view as well. Now type a simple # (hash symbol) into the *Link* text box in the *Properties* palette window. Notice how some new code surrounding the selected word in the upper section has been added—this is the link code which we will edit next.

6 Click just inside the end of the tag (the text surrounded by the angle brackets) just before the word you selected; after the quotation mark but before the closing angle bracket. Now type

onMouseOver="javascript: changeBackground(1)"

into the code. This defines the trigger (onMouseOver) and tells the browser that the instruction to perform is JavaScript. Finally, the 'changeBackground' function is called, with a number to define what "backgroundColor" to use. Use the same code for the "what?" text, substituting (0) instead of (1) in the code.

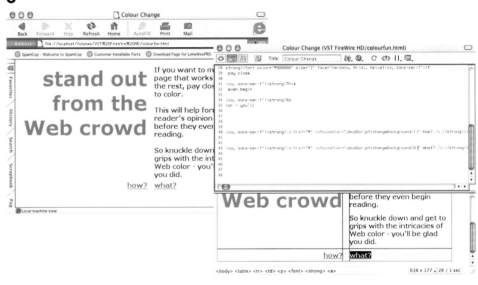

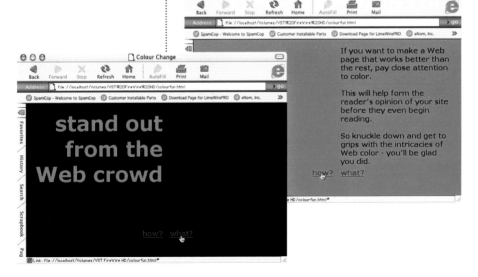

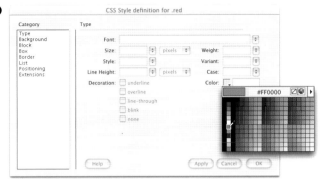

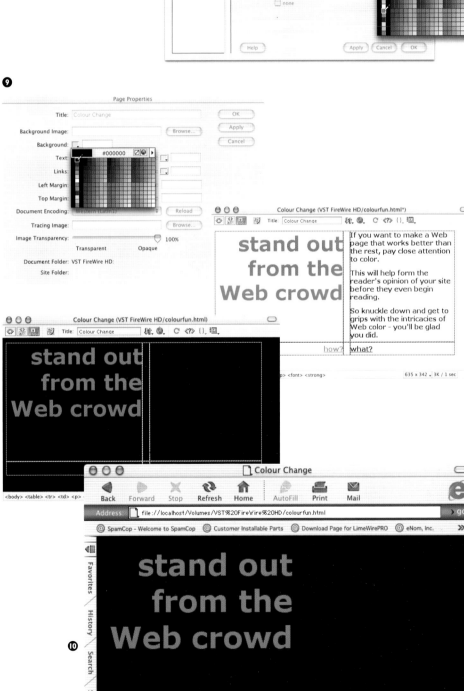

7 When you try this page out in a browser, you will see the page color change when you point at each link. You will also notice a couple of other things: the initial default white page color does not hide the black text, and the two links are the default link blue.

8 To polish this off, we need to make two new CSS styles, one red and one black, and make the standard page color black. Go to the *Text* menu, down to *CSS Styles*, and choose *New CSS Style*. Call it "black," then set the color to black using the color pop-up picker. Next, make another CSS style, call it "red," and give it a red color.

9 Now select the "how?" text and apply the red CSS style by going to the *Text* menu and picking it from the *CSS Styles* list. Then make the "what?" text black in the same way. Finally, set the page background to black by choosing *Page Properties* from the *Modify* menu and picking black from the pop-up colors picker.

10 Now your page is ready to hide and show different elements by changing the background color. This trick takes a small amount of fiddling with code, but you will probably agree that the final result is quite effective.

50 PROJECT 5
ANIMATED BACKGROUND COLORS

As well as switching from one background color to another like flicking a switch, it is possible to animate a color change so that it cycles smoothly from one shade to the next. This makes for a much softer end result, which can be much more suitable for certain website designs. What is actually happening behind the scenes is a simple series of color switches, but because it goes through many hues and colors, with only subtle changes in each step, the cycle from beginning to end feels smooth.

This trick does involve using a rather large amount of JavaScript code. You can copy the code from our example pages at www.webexpertseries.com/color, then paste and tweak it using Dreamweaver or GoLive. If you use a Macintosh computer, this is much more easily handled in Freeway, using the *Background Fade* action.

Actions are plug-in files that extend the main program in many ways. A wide selection of actions are included as standard, but for this project you'll need to download a custom action from the Softpress site. Get online and point your browser at www.softpress.com/actions. Click the *Actions Library* link, then pick the A-E set. In that list, you'll find *Background Fade*; download that file and put it into the Freeway Actions folder inside your main Freeway program folder. While you are on the Softpress site, you might also want to find and download the *Background Image* action; this cycles the page background between as many as six different colors.

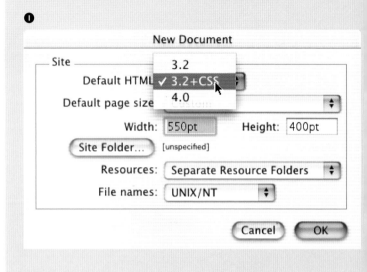

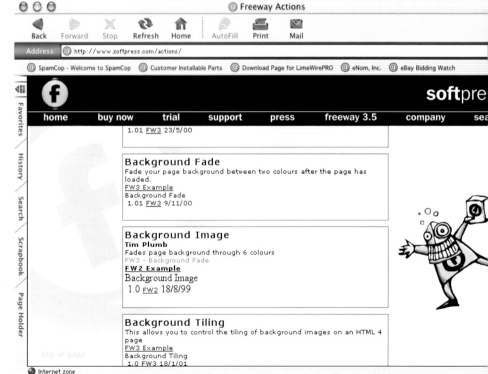

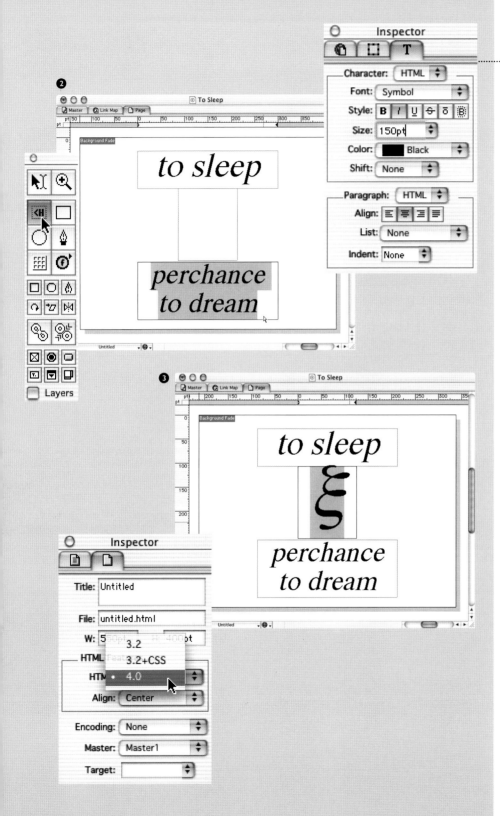

❶ Make a new document in Freeway, with the page size set to 550x400 and the Default HTML set to either 3.2+CSS or 4.0. The page size is purely to help with the design process; it doesn't force the browser window to a specific size.

❷ Draw out three HTML text boxes using the tool button immediately below the arrow button in the *Tools* palette. Place them in a vertical stack (hold down the Apple key to grab and move them easily), then click on each in turn to add the text. The top and bottom ones are set with Times italic (click the "I" button in the *Inspector* palette), and the size is set to 72 points (type 72 into the Size box).

❸ The box between these two has a single character, a letter "w" set using the Symbol typeface, also italic, but with the size set to 150 points. If you can't set the size to points just by typing the number and pressing return, click on an empty part of the page, then double check that the *Inspector* palette shows HTML set to 3.2+CSS or 4.0. If it is set to 3.2, you need to change it.

52

④ Make sure that nothing is selected, then pick a dark night-time blue from the colors shown in the second panel of the *Styles* palette. This sets the page color. Now select the top portion of text and pick a pale gray; set the middle character to be a mid-gray; and the bottom text to be a darker blue than the background. If you pick exactly the same colors as we have your page will look like this.

⑤ Now we will take things a step further by making the page background color change by cycling from one color to another over a few seconds. The JavaScript involved in performing this is quite hefty, but luckily the *Background Fade* action takes care of most of the work for us. Go to the *Page* menu and slide down to *Actions*, then pick *Background Fade* from the list.

⑥ To pick the start and end colors and set the duration of the crossfade, choose *Actions* from the *Window* menu. Now, from the *Actions* window pick the start and end colors from the pop-up lists. Set the interval to 2, and set the number of steps to 30. This makes the change run at about fifteen steps per second; just about enough to give the viewer a sense of smooth cycling.

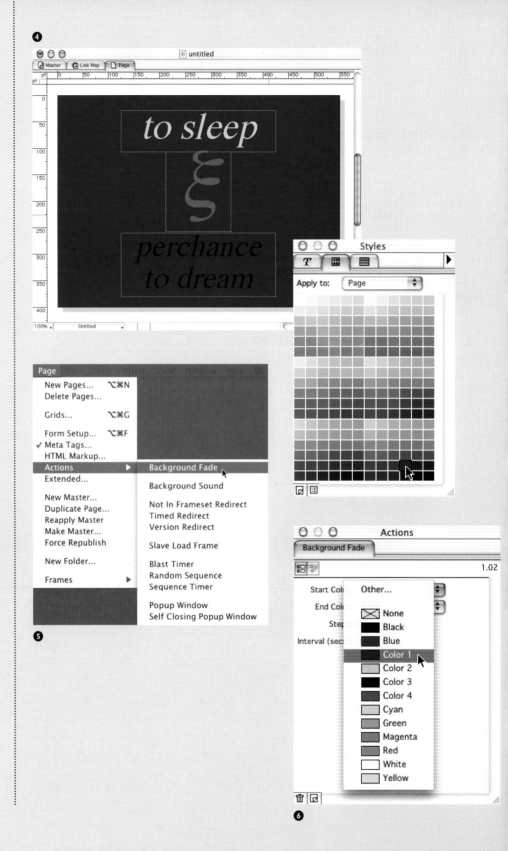

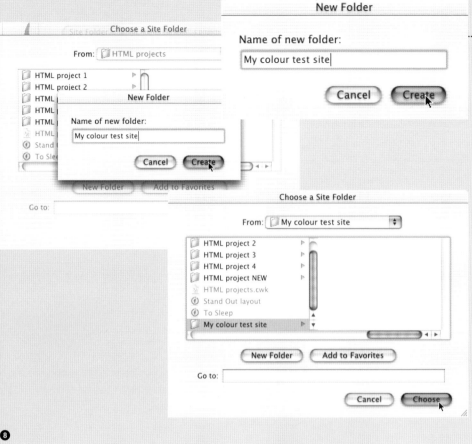

New Folder

Name of new folder:

My colour test site

Cancel   Create

⑦ To see how this works, you will need to preview it in a Web browser. Go to the *File* menu and pick a browser from the *Preview* list. As this particular document hasn't been previewed before, you will have to tell Freeway where to store the HTML code it is about to make for you. Create a new folder, then click the *Choose* button to pick it.

⑧ Your default Web browser will load and your page will open in it. The color change will happen automatically over about two seconds, changing the visual focus from one part of the text to another. This is a much more gentle kind of change than the standard rollover color switching, although, as set up here, it will only happen when the page is loaded. Click your browser's refresh button if you want to see it happen again.

54 PROJECT 6
USING LAYERS AS DESIGN ELEMENTS

Layers enable all sorts of clever and useful things to be done that simply cannot be achieved using normal "flat" HTML. For instance, as you have probably noticed during these projects, it isn't possible to overlap HTML items in a layout. These basic HTML structures are positioned on the page using table grid structures, and there is simply no ability to stack things up. If layers are used, however, this all changes. You can put some text into a layer, then place it on top of other text. A headline can be positioned part-way off from a block of color for dramatic effect, or pushed right over the edge of an image. The use of layers also enables a more reliable positioning of items; table structures can be messed around a little by text sizes working differently in different Web browsers, but layers are totally independent entities on the page.

Do be aware that not all browsers handle layers particularly well. By now, the majority of people using the Web will be using a Web browser that can cope with layers, but there is still a small percentage of Web users that run old, less-capable software. On top of this, "special needs" browsers—such as screen readers for the visually impaired—and some of the new generations of PDA-based browsers are not likely to present layers well, if at all. You will have to decide which projects would benefit from using such techniques, and whether that would affect the kind of person you are aiming your site at. All the same, don't be put off from using such a marvelous box of tricks.

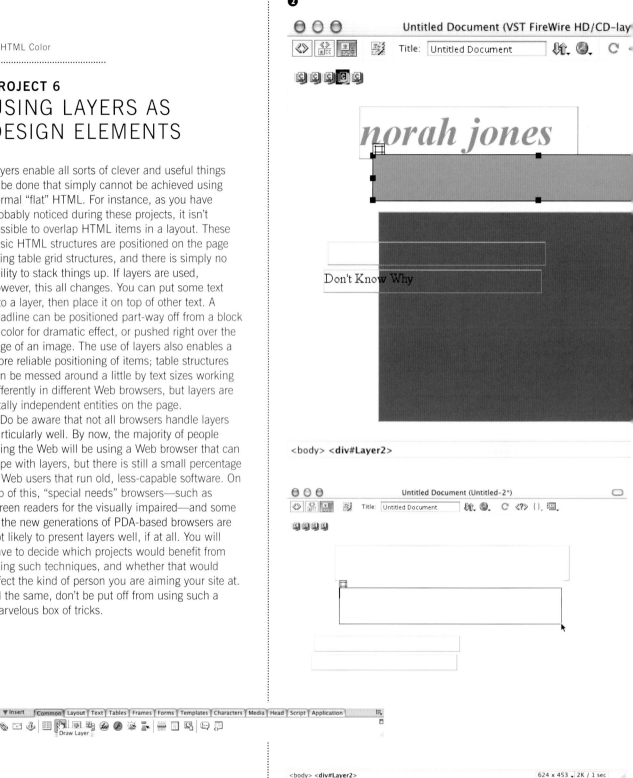

❸ Modify

Page Properties...	⌘J
Template Properties...	
✓ Selection Properties	⇧⌘J
Edit Tag...	
Quick Tag Editor	⌘T
Make Link	⌘L
Remove Link	⇧⌘L
Open Linked Page...	
Link Target	▶
Table	▶
Frameset	▶
Navigation Bar	
Arrange	▶
Align	▶
Convert	▶
Library	▶
Templates	▶
Timeline	▶

Bring To Front
Send To Back

Prevent Layer Overlaps

❹

○ ○ ○ Untitled Document (VST FireWire HD/CD-layers.html*)

Title: Untitled Document

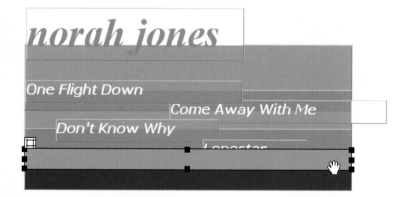

norah jones

One Flight Down

Come Away With Me

Don't Know Why

Lonestar

<body> <div#Layer2>   624 x 453 ⬚ 4K / 1 s

❶ **Dreamweaver** First of all, we will make a few layer items to work with in our page. Click the *Draw Layer* icon in the *Insert* toolbar, and draw out layer boxes in the page. Each new layer also creates a new *Layer Marker* icon at the top of the page. These don't show in the Web page; they merely help the designer keep track of the items on the page.

❷ Click inside layers to type text, and format the text by selecting and styling as usual. Select a layer by clicking on its edge, or by clicking the correct *Layer Marker* item in the top of the page, then resize and drag it into position. Use the pop-up color picker in the *Properties* palette to fill complete layer items with color.

❸ Here the layer used as the title is stacked behind the top color block layer; it was created first, so the newer items sit on top of it. To send a layer behind another, select it, then go to *Arrange* in the *Modify* menu and pick *Send To Back*. This doesn't affect the order of the *Layer Marker* items, just the stacking order of the objects as they are displayed in Dreamweaver or the browser.

❹ The title graphic sits snugly on the top color block, and different text layers are placed on the division between different layer blocks. Dragging items around will get things more or less into position, but for pixel-perfect placement watch the L (left), T (top), W (width), and H (height) text boxes in the *Properties* palette to see if the element selected is spot on or one pixel out. The narrow bars are all 400 pixels wide by 24 pixels tall, and 90 pixels from the left edge of the window.

56

5 Now we will add another text layer and nudge it right underneath the main title. Draw out a new layer, anywhere on the page, then drag it underneath the large text. Click inside and type the text shown here. This layout is based on two different shades (a moderately light blue and a shaded violet), designed to complement the subject, but for this text use a white to "punch through" to the page color.

6 One small detail is missing now: the dot on the "i" in the word "with." It is still there of course, but as it is white on white, it cannot be seen. The tops of the letters "t" and "h" are also lost, but we won't worry about them for the moment.

7 Draw out another layer item (just a small one) and drag it near the problem word. Type a dot into the box, then style it to match the white text—except, of course, for the color. Instead of white, we will make it blue to match the layer color behind the white text. Drag it into position to make the word look more or less as it should.

To see if the dot is positioned properly, go to *Page Properties* in the *Modify* menu and set the page color to something other than white. Now everything should show up clearly and you can place the item more precisely. Remember to set the page color back to either "no color" or white afterward.

8 Take a look at how a Web browser displays your work. You may find that there are slight differences in the way text is shown, even with layers holding things in place. Also, unless you were particularly careful when placing things in step 4, you will probably notice a few

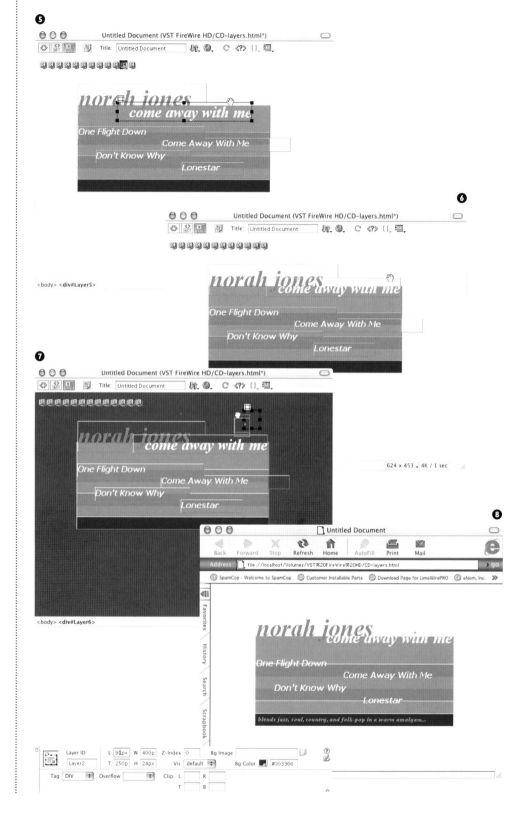

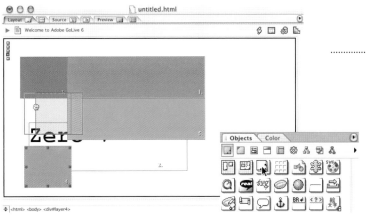

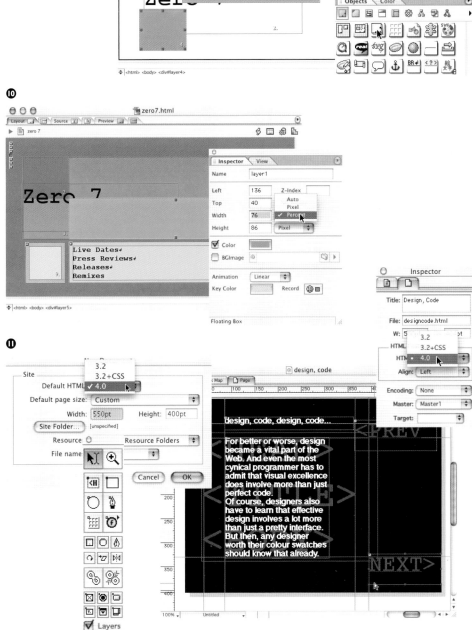

slightly misaligned items. Try nudging things around to fine-tune your work; select a misaligned item and nudge it using the keyboard arrow keys, or type exact coordinates into the *Properties* palette.

⑨ GoLive Layer objects are known as "floating boxes" in GoLive; create these by dragging the *Floating Box* item from the *Objects* palette into the page. From there, you can click on their edges to reshape and reposition them. The tiny yellow icons shown in the page are much the same as the layer markers in Dreamweaver, but in GoLive you change the stacking order of objects by dragging the yellow icons into a variety of different arrangements. The number in the bottom right corner of the layer shows its placement in the stack.

⑩ Set the color of floating box items using the *Inspector* palette as normal. This also shows the numeric size and position information for the selected object; just edit this to get a precise layout. GoLive also provides scaling options for floating box items; pick *Percent* to have the selected item scale up and down with the page size. As you can see, using layers (or floating boxes) offers a lot to the creative designer.

⑪ Freeway In Freeway, items can be converted to and from layer objects by clicking the *Layer* checkbox in the *Inspector* palette. First, however, the page's HTML setting must be set at HTML 4.0 (check and make sure). If you plan to create a lot of layer items, click the *Layers* checkbox in the Tools palette before making them. In this case, objects will be handled as layers automatically.

58
PROJECT 7
INTERACTIVE
LAYER EFFECTS

Layers are not restricted to sitting around on the
page—they can also be dragged around. This is not
something that you will need to do a lot, but it does
offer very interesting ways to play with color
juxtapositions. (It can also lend itself to things like
example layouts, where the user gets to try placing
headlines, pictures, and blocks of text in different
arrangements.)

This trick uses
a Dreamweaver
"behavior": a canned
instruction that sets
up complex JavaScript
instructions in an
HTML page, a little
like Freeway's simpler
actions. Without this,
designers would have
to resort to writing
their own JavaScript
or figuring out how to
adapt someone else's
scripts for their own
use. There is nothing
wrong with that, but
it takes time away
from the actual design
task. Use behaviors
whenever you can
rather than doing
things the hard way.

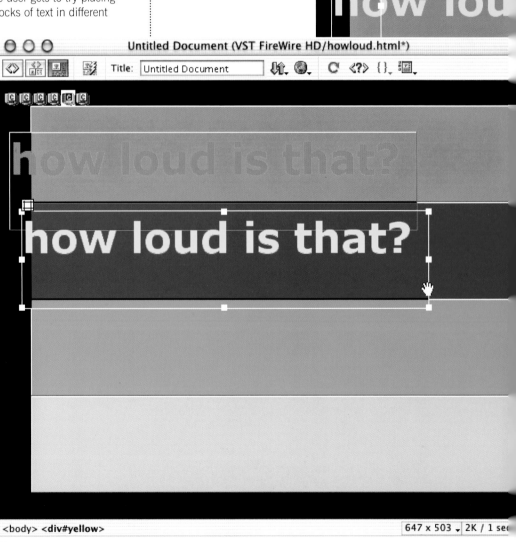

●

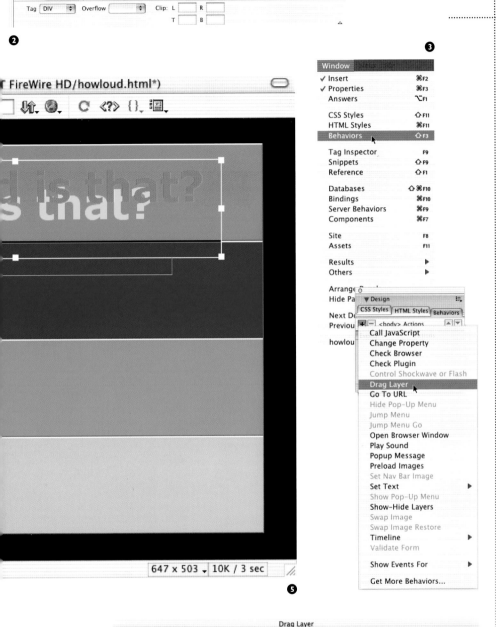

❶ Make six layers in a new Dreamweaver document, and fill four with strong colors—pure HTML red (#FF0000), green (#00FF00), blue (#0000FF), and a "video" cyan (00FFFF). Stack them vertically down the page and type "How loud is that?" into both the final two layers. Set the text to be the largest regular type size, bold, and Verdana. Finally, color one lot of text a shocking pink (#FF00FF) and the other a bright yellow (#FFFF00).

❷ Using the *Properties* palette, change the layer ID of the yellow text layer to "yellow" and the ID of the pink text layer to "pink." This will make it much simpler to know which is which.

❸ Now choose *Behaviors* from the *Window* menu. Make sure that nothing is selected before trying this next step. In the small floating window with the *Behaviors* tab, click the *Plus* button and pick *Drag Layer* from the menu that appears. If you cannot select this item, make sure that no item is selected and try again.

❹ Once the *Drag Layer* dialog appears, pick the "yellow" layer, then pick *Constrained* from the *Movement* pop-up menu, and type a zero in the *Left* and the *Right* text boxes. This prevents the layer from moving left or right when dragged, relative to its position in the Dreamweaver layout. Pick *Drag Layer* from the *Behaviors* menu again and repeat for the "pink" layer.

❺ Position the two text layers carefully—they can be dragged only up and down in the Web browser, not left and right. Also consider where they are on the page, because that's where the viewer will see them first.

60

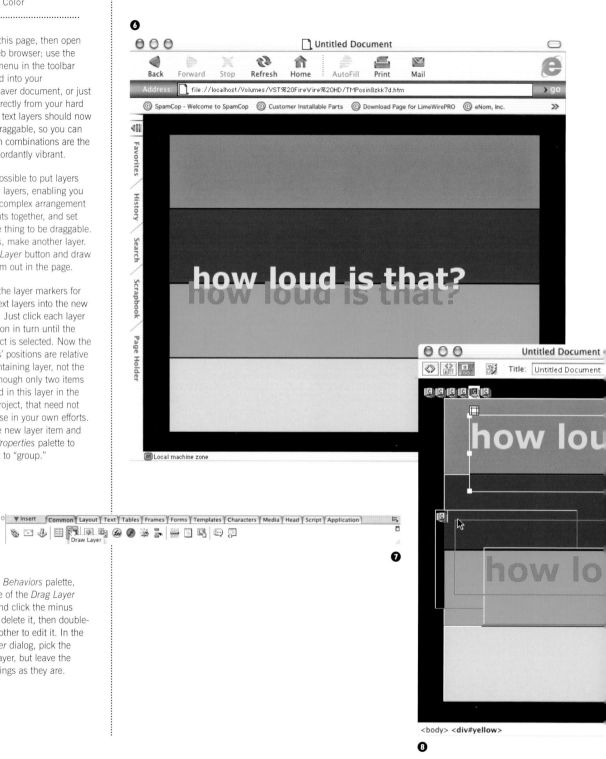

6 Save this page, then open it in a Web browser; use the *Preview* menu in the toolbar embedded into your Dreamweaver document, or just open it directly from your hard disk. The text layers should now be fully draggable, so you can see which combinations are the most discordantly vibrant.

7 It is possible to put layers into other layers, enabling you to lock a complex arrangement of elements together, and set the whole thing to be draggable. To try this, make another layer. Click the *Layer* button and draw a new item out in the page.

8 Drag the layer markers for the two text layers into the new layer box. Just click each layer marker icon in turn until the right object is selected. Now the two items' positions are relative to the containing layer, not the page. Although only two items are placed in this layer in the current project, that need not be the case in your own efforts. Select the new layer item and use the *Properties* palette to rename it to "group."

9 In the *Behaviors* palette, select one of the *Drag Layer* actions and click the minus button to delete it, then double-click the other to edit it. In the *Drag Layer* dialog, pick the "group" layer, but leave the other settings as they are.

10 Now resize the container layer so that it covers the area a user would expect to be able to grab, and place it where you want the words to appear. Preview the page and drag the words around again—the result should be even more eye-searing than before!

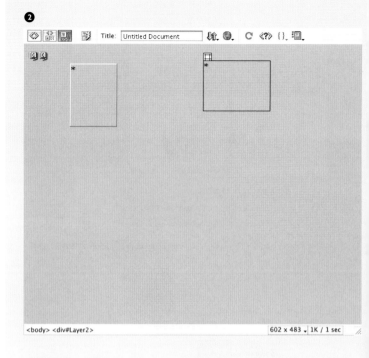

62 PROJECT 8

ANIMATING LAYERS USING A TIMELINE

Layers can also be moved from one place to another over a period of time, whatever they may hold. This is done using a combination of JavaScript and Cascading Style Sheets (CSS)—or Dynamic HTML (DHTML), as many like to call it. Dreamweaver offers a particularly good timeline feature with easy controls for automatically starting and looping animations as well as setting animation keyframes (the main points of an animation) for objects.

This isn't to be confused with the serious Web animation effects achieved using tools such as Macromedia Flash or Adobe Live Motion, but it does work directly with the code that makes up the HTML page. No plug-ins are required, just a Web browser that understands frames and DHTML—in other words, the majority of browsers in use today.

As with all animation tasks it can take some time to get things just right, so practice until you feel comfortable with the concepts involved.

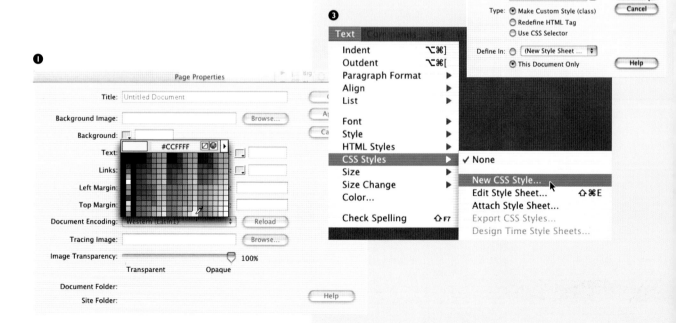

❹

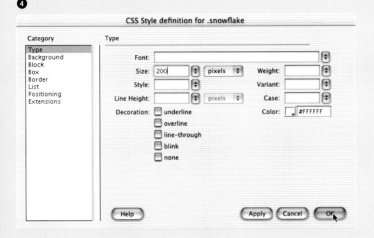

❺

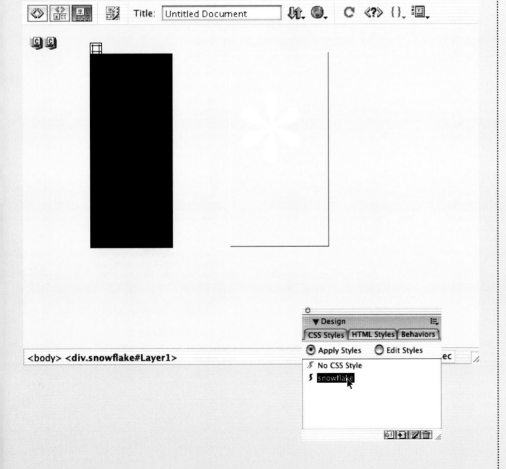

`<body> <div.snowflake#Layer1>`

❶ Start by making a new page in Dreamweaver, then setting the page color to a cool, pale blue: choose *Page Properties* in the *Modify* menu, then choose an appropriate color from the Background color picker. HTML color #CCFFFF is a particularly good choice.

❷ Drag a couple of floating box objects into the page from the *Objects* palette, then move them apart so that you can see them separately at the top of the page. Now type an asterisk (*) into each. We're going to use these layers as snowflakes, with Dreamweaver's *Timeline* controller animating them falling down the page. We will need a few more snowflakes later on, but two is enough to get started.

❸ Basic HTML text formatting is not able to give us the large text sizes we need for this to be effective, so a CSS style will have to be made. This will format text to any size we like. In the *Text* menu, go to *CSS Styles* and pick *New CSS Style*. Call this style "snowflake."

❹ In the *CSS Style* dialog, choose white from the *Color* list, and type "200" into the *Size* text box. Make sure the size type is set to pixels in the pop-up menu next to the *Size* box.

❺ Now choose *CSS Styles* from the *Window* menu. You will see the "snowflake" style listed; select one of the asterisks in the page and click this style. The asterisk is now very large and white. Repeat this with the other one and you have a chilly pale blue "sky" with a couple of large snowflakes sitting there. You are now ready to use the *Timeline* window.

6 In the *Window* menu, go to *Others* and pick *Timelines*. This opens the *Timeline* window, where you can add layer objects and animate them over time. To put a layer item into the *Timeline* window, just drag it over. Put both items in, one below the other.

7 Click on the final cell of one of the timeline objects, and drag the layer item in the page down to the bottom of the window. When you let go, you will see a line stretching from its original spot to the new position. Do this to the second item as well, then drag the red playbar marker back and forth to see the objects animate in your page.

8 Slide the playbar back to the beginning of the timeline. Then, in the page, click on each layer in turn and drag it up so that the asterisk is almost off the top of the page. Now when you drag through the timeline, the white "snowflakes" will appear at the top of the cold blue page.

9 How about making the snowflakes appear to swirl about a little rather than fall in a straight line? Select one of the layer bars in the timeline, somewhere near the middle, then either right-click or Control-click the bar and choose *Add keyframe* from the menu that appears.

10 Now drag the layer on the page to a different position. You will see the timeline path bend to show the new path the object will take. Add a few more layers and put giant asterisks in each one, then put them into the timeline and animate a small snow flurry. Make the animation paths cross over to make the effect more complex and convincing overall.

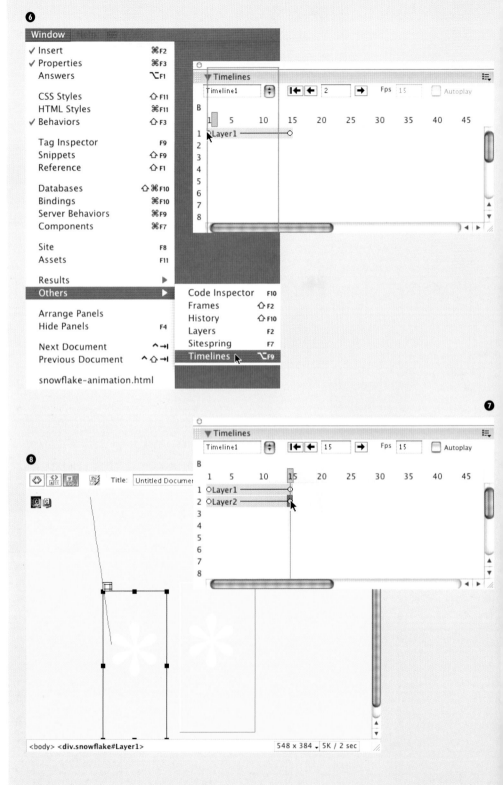

9

Having finished this project, you might notice that all the snowflake layers appear at once in a bit of a clump. To make things happen at different times, simply drag their timeline bars to different horizontal positions; drag some to finish at frame 30, and others at earlier frames. You can also extend or compress the time an item takes to play through by dragging the beginning or end point to a different spot in the timeline. And finally, *Copy* and *Paste* timeline items to duplicate them in your animation.

Click the *Autoplay* and the *Loop* checkboxes in the *Timeline* window. (You may need to open the *Timeline* window out a little to see the *Loop* checkbox.) This makes the animation start playing automatically when the page is shown in a Web browser, and keep looping from start to end, over and over.

You may also wish to add a few animated layers that start in the middle of the page and go off by halfway through, as well as matching layers that appear at the top in the middle of the sequence and end up in the middle of the page by the end of the timeline. This helps to hide the beginning and end of the animation sequence quite effectively, giving the effect of a continuously moving background.

10

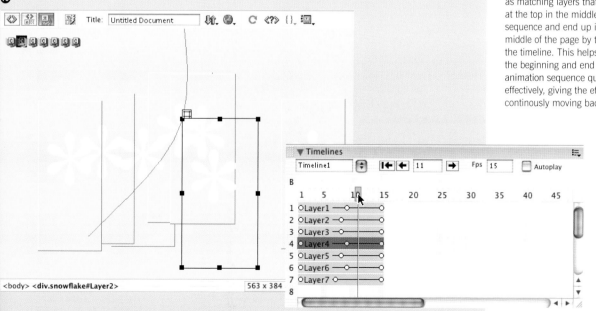

66 **PROJECT 9**

HIDING AND SHOWING LAYERS USING TIMELINES

Moving layers about over time is not the only thing you can do with a timeline feature. You can also hide and show elements at different places in the timeline, whether they are flying about or sitting still in one spot. For example, you can make a flashing text banner or simulate a flickering neon sign. This project builds directly on the previous task, so make sure you were happy with what you made there. This one shouldn't take long to complete, as you should have grasped the main concept already. But don't rush it—layers and timelines can still be fiddly things to manipulate.

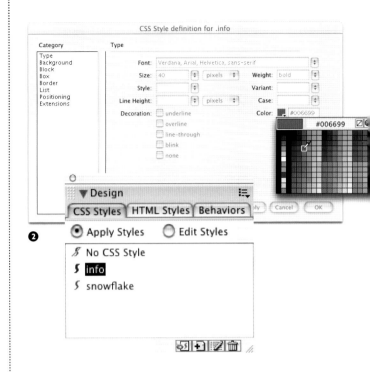

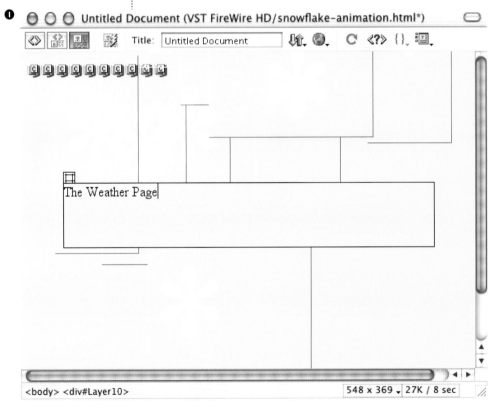

❸

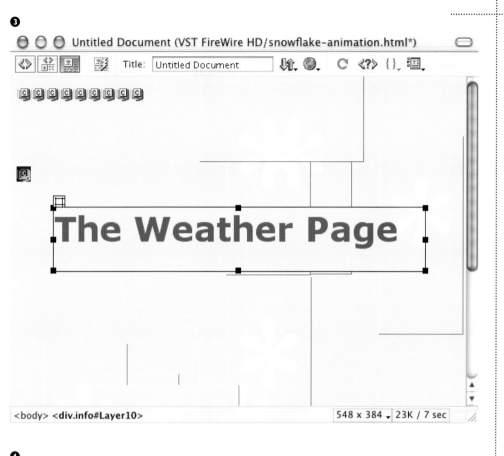

❹

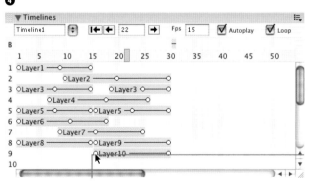

❶ Open up the previous project. To add a banner, which appears briefly during the animation. First, make a new layer item. Click the *Layer* button in the *Insert* toolbar and draw the layer item out somewhere near the middle of the page. Type "The Weather Page" in this new layer.

❷ In the *Type* menu, go to *CSS Styles* and choose *New CSS Style*. Name it "info" and click OK. Then set the font to Verdana, the size to 40 pixels, the weight to bold, and the color to #006699. This will now appear as an entry in the *CSS Styles* palette—choose *CSS Styles* from the *Window* menu if the palette is not visible.

❸ Select the text in your new layer and apply the "info" CSS style by clicking it in the *CSS Styles* palette. Your page should now look like this.

❹ If the *Timeline* window isn't open, pick it from the *Others* item in the *Window* menu. Drag the new layer into the *Timeline* window. The position doesn't actually matter, as we are doing this only to place it under the *Timeline*'s control.

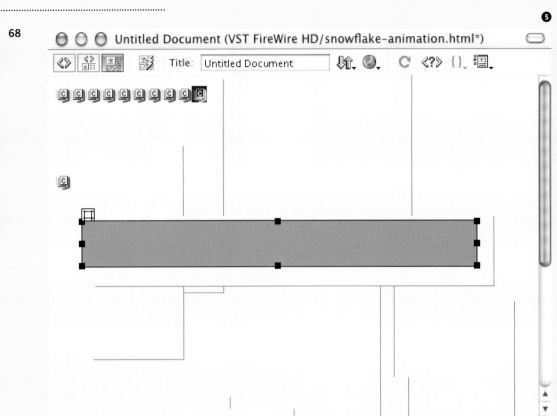

❻

Modify

Page Properties...	⌘J
Template Properties...	
✓ Selection Properties	⇧⌘J
Edit Tag...	
Quick Tag Editor	⌘T
Make Link	⌘L
Remove Link	⇧⌘L
Open Linked Page...	
Link Target	▶
Table	▶
Frameset	▶
Navigation Bar	
Arrange	▶
Align	▶
Convert	▶
Library	▶
Templates	▶
Timeline	▶

Bring To Front
Send To Back

Prevent Layer Overlaps

▼ Design

CSS Styles   HTML Styles   Behaviors

⊞ − <timeline> Actions   ▲ ▼

Call JavaScript
Change Property
Check Browser
Check Plugin
Control Shockwave or Flash
Drag Layer
Go To URL
Hide Pop-Up Menu
Jump Menu
Jump Menu Go
Open Browser Window
Play Sound
Popup Message
Preload Images
Set Nav Bar Image
Set Text   ▶
Show Pop-Up Menu
Show-Hide Layers
Swap Image
Swap Image Restore
Timeline   ▶
Validate Form

Show Events For   ▶

Get More Behaviors...

❼

▼ Timelines

Timeline1 ⬍ |← ← 1   ☑ Loop

B ▮

1   5   10   15   20   25   30   35   40   45   50

1 ○Layer1 ——○———○
2   ○Layer2 ———○———○
3 ○Layer3 ——○   ○Layer3 ——○———○
4   ○Layer4 ———○
5 ○Layer5 ——○   ○○Layer5 ——○———○
6 ○Layer6 ———○———○
7   ○Layer7 ———○———○
8 ○Layer8 ————○○Layer9 ———————○

❽

Show-Hide Layers

Named Layers: layer "Layer8"   OK
               layer "Layer9"
               layer "Layer11" (hide)   Cancel
               layer "Layer10"
                                            Help

Show   Hide   Default

❺ Draw out another layer on top of the text. This will be a banner-style box behind the words, so make it sit fairly snugly around the text. Now use the color picker in the *Properties* palette to fill its background with a shady aquamarine (HTML color #666699.)

❻ Put this box behind the other layers by choosing *Arrange* from the *Modify* menu and picking *Send To Back*. Drag it into the *Timeline* window immediately underneath the text layer.

❼ The top row in the *Timeline*, the one marked with a B—is where behaviors are stored. Click in the first cell in the row, then go to the *Behaviors* palette window. Click the plus button and choose *Show-Hide* from the menu that appears.

❽ Scroll down to the last two items and set them to be hidden, then click OK. Now go to cell 15 in the *Behavior* row and add another *Show-Hide* behavior. This time, set the final layer, the colored block, to be shown. Then click in cell 21 in the *Behavior* row and use *Show-Hide* to show the text layer. Finally, go to the last cell in the animation and add a behavior to set both the colored block and the text layers to be hidden. Just preview the page or load it into your Web browser to see the finished effect.

PROJECT 10

PLAYING WITH FRAMES: A "MONDRIAN EFFECT"

Frames take more than one Web page document and show them within separate sections of a window. In fact, think of it as a window with a number of different panes, or frames. The frameset is the overall structure, and each frame within that frameset can show a different page. You can also show the same page in more than one frame at once, if you would rather.

This GoLive project takes a stab at recreating a classic 1932 painting by Mondrian, called *Composition with Blue and Yellow*. It then plays with a trick that the original could not possibly match—changing sections of the frameset automatically while the viewer watches. The result is not great art, but it should teach you a lot about frame-based designs.

❶ This project involves working with a number of different pages. To make things a little easier, we will begin by choosing *New Site* instead of *New Page* from the *File* menu in GoLive. Tell GoLive you are a single user and that you want a "blank site." Call it "Mondrian," and pick a folder for the site— make a new one if necessary.

You will end up with a new site window, which lists all the parts of your site. So far, this contains just one page, "index.html," but it will soon have several more.

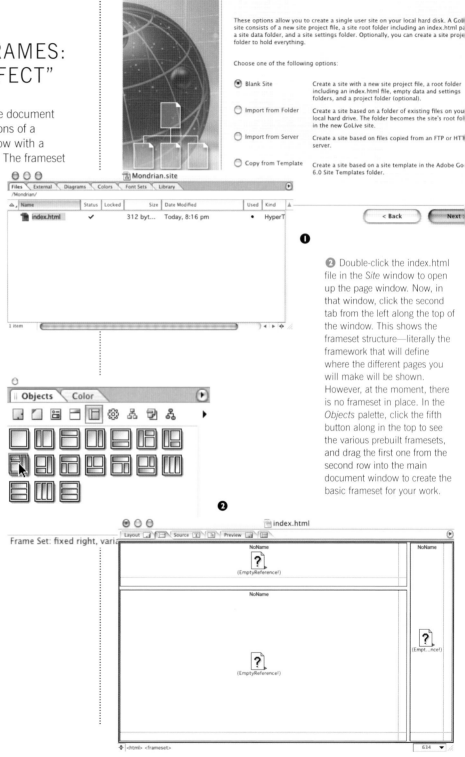

❷ Double-click the index.html file in the *Site* window to open up the page window. Now, in that window, click the second tab from the left along the top of the window. This shows the frameset structure—literally the framework that will define where the different pages you will make will be shown. However, at the moment, there is no frameset in place. In the *Objects* palette, click the fifth button along in the top to see the various prebuilt framesets, and drag the first one from the second row into the main document window to create the basic frameset for your work.

❸

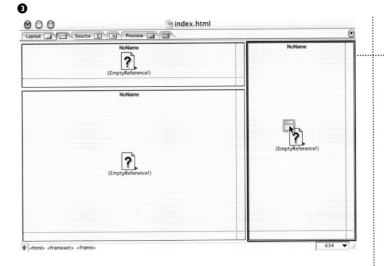

❹

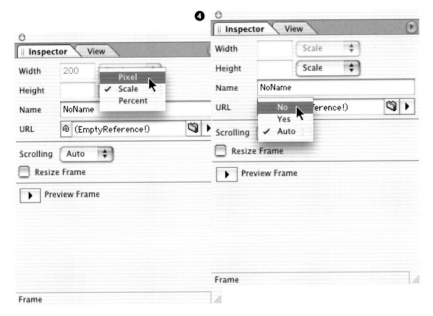

❺

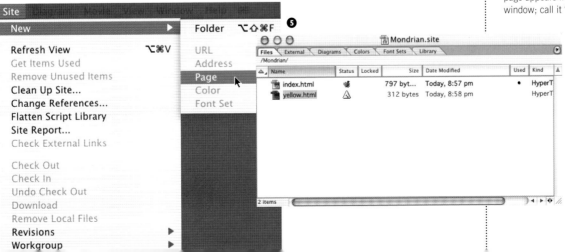

❸ To make the construction that we are after, drag another frameset icon from the *Objects* palette into the right-hand vertical frame. If needed, drag out the central divider bar to the left to give you more room. Use the third along from the top row —although this claims to make two frames, it actually produces three when dropped in, and that is actually what we want.

❹ Click in the upper-right frame. This is currently set to grow when the window is made larger, but we need it to be exactly 200 pixels tall. In the *Inspector* palette, choose *Pixel* instead of *Scale* from the *Height* pop-up menu, then type 200 in the text box. Now click in the frame immediately below and make it 200 pixels tall. Click the border between the top two cells on the right so you see a black line surrounding the entire vertical set of three frames, and set the width to 190 pixels. Now make the top frame 200 pixels high. Finally, click in each frame in turn and pick *No* from the *Scrolling* choices in the *Inspector* palette.

❺ Now you need to make the individual pages that will be shown in each frame. Click on the *Site* window, then go to the *Site* menu and slide down to *New*, then pick *Page*. A new page appears in the *Site* window; call it "yellow.html."

72

⑥ Double-click the new "yellow.html" page, then go to the *Special* menu and pick *Page Properties*. This shows the *Page* panel in the *Inspector* palette. Make sure *Background* is checked, then click the color button and pick a slightly dusky yellow from the *Color* palette. You are quite limited in Web-safe HTML colors, so feel free to pick a different color mixer option from the array at the top of the palette. Using the RGB color sliders, you can choose 255 red, 241 green, and 50 blue (color #FFF232 in hexadecimal). Now close this page, saving when prompted.

⑦ Make another page, call it "blue.html," then open it and color it blue. We used red 0, green 80, and blue 125, (#00507D). Now make a third page and call it "white.html," then color it white. Close and save both pages.

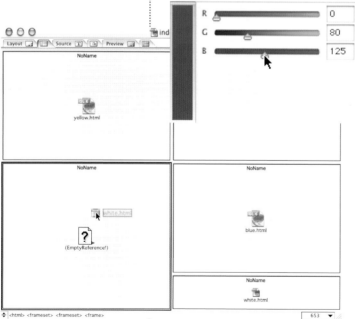

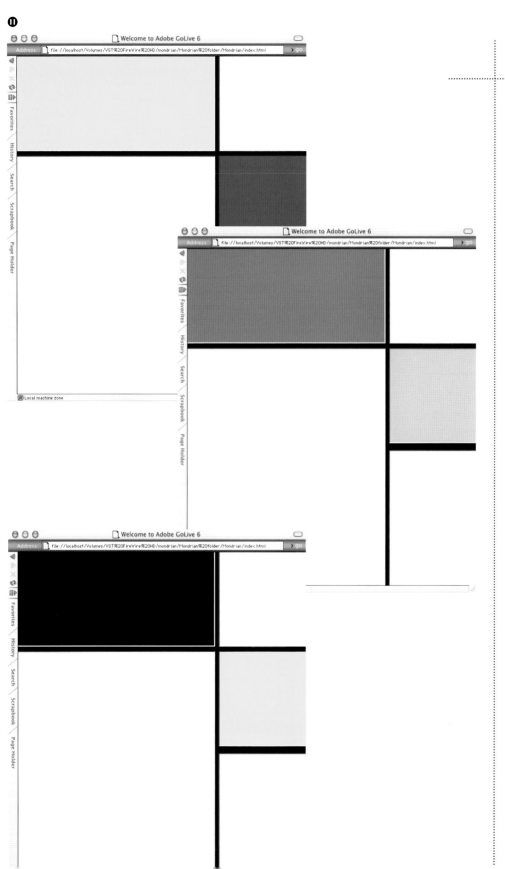

8 Drag the "yellow.html" page from the site window into the upper left frame in the frameset window, the "blue.html" page into the middle right frame, and the "white.html" page into the other three frames. Click the last tab on the right at the top of your document to get a preview.

9 Click back into the regular frame view (second tab from the left), then click the vertical bar in the middle. Now go to the *Inspector* palette and turn on all three border options: *BorderSize*, *BorderColor*, and *BorderFrame*. Set *BorderSize* to 8 pixels, and make the color black. If you pick *No* from the frame options to eliminate the 3D sculpted look, the frame color disappears in some browsers, so ignore this option. If you now click on other frame bars, you will be able to set the thickness individually.

10 Now create some more pages, coloring them red (#CC0000), gray (#CCCCCC), and black (#000000). Open all of the "colored" pages (not index.html) and, in the *Objects* palette, click the fourth button from the left. This is the *Head* button. Drag the *Refresh* object into each page.

11 For each page, go to the *Inspector* palette and click the *Target URL* button, then type a different page name into the text box. It must be one of the other "color" pages, and you must use the full name (including .html). Change the delay time for each page; save and close all pages; then open index.html and click the *Show In Browser* button in the main toolbar.

Each page now has a timer. When it runs out, the named page is loaded into the frame for a cycling Mondrian effect!

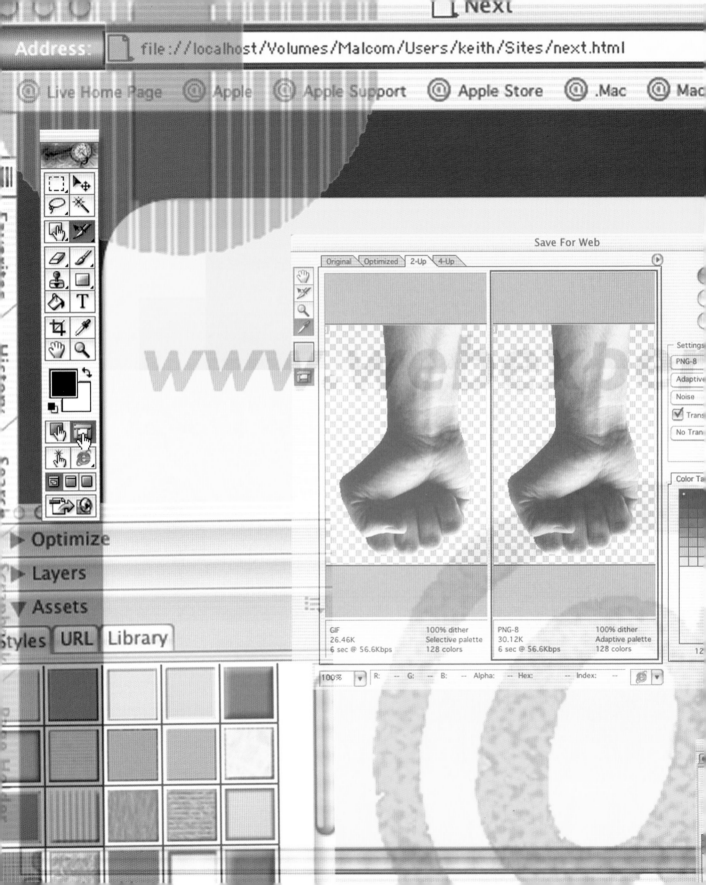

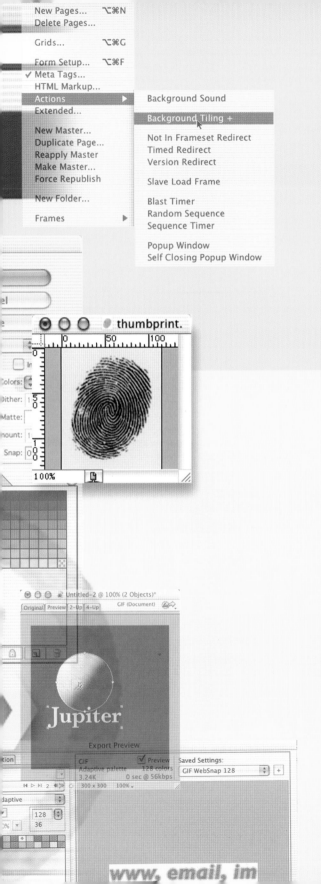

C H A P T E R 4

Bitmap Color

Working with graphics is a key part of Web design. Creating and optimizing images to fit into specific color schemes takes practice, but it really isn't hard. This chapter starts with the basics of using Web-safe and custom colors in images, before demonstrating antialiasing tricks, image compression and more. Then projects on color reduction and selective blurring show how to force file sizes down without ruining the colors in your image.

Other projects reveal the possibilities offered by graphic transparency, plus the many different ways of putting still and animated images into colored backgrounds. The results are bound to stop viewers dead in their tracks.

PROJECT 11
OPTIMIZING GIFS

One of the oldest building blocks of Web design, GIF graphics are perfect for flat color graphics such as line illustrations, buttons, and graphic text. It isn't the most versatile file format around—as it can handle only a limited palette of 256 colors, the GIF format is not ideal for photographic content—but most of the limitations can be worked around if handled with care.

Optimizing an image for GIF use involves reducing the number of colors it uses. The fewer colors a GIF file uses, the simpler it is to describe, and the less space it takes on your disk. This translates to shorter download times for someone reading it from a Web page. If too few colors are used, however, the image can become patchy and unrealistic. In the case of a basic text graphic, this is simple enough to handle. But when more realistic photographic or illustrated elements are involved, it becomes critical to pick the right balance between file size and the appearance.

Apart from a small file size, the most useful feature that the GIF file format can offer is transparency. This is simple "one-bit" transparency, where a single flat color is nominated as the one to be made invisible, with no partial translucent-style transparency. Despite this constraint, transparent GIFs are perfect for cutouts over a colored or textured background— for example, chunky display text; site navigation buttons; or simple product photos with the background removed.

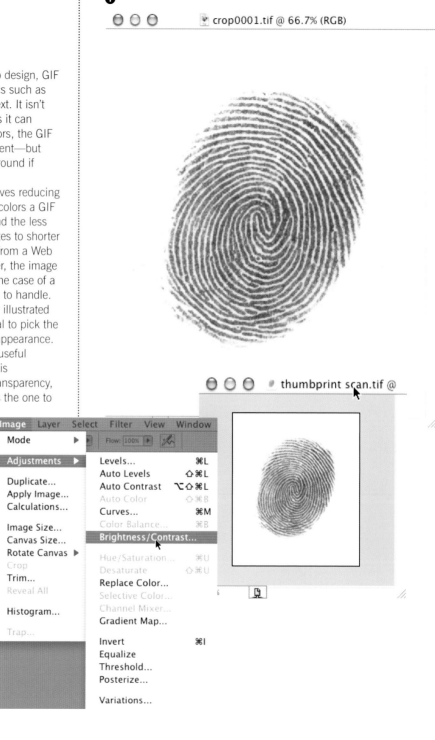

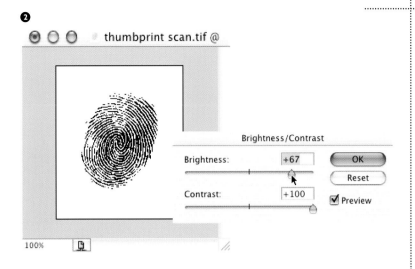

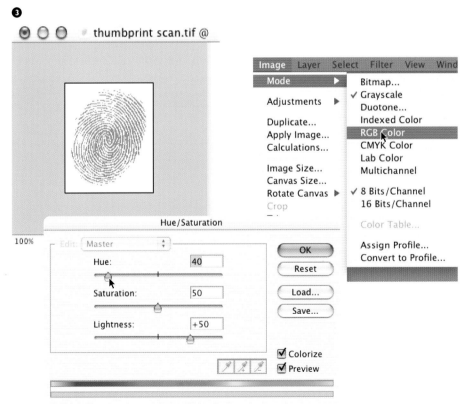

❶ This scan of a thumbprint will be used to "brand" a Web page. It was made by scanning a simple print made on paper, so first it needs to be optimized. This is supposed to be a very stark, high-contrast image, so set the brightness and contrast levels to get rid of any midtone grays. In Photoshop or Photoshop Elements, scale the image (*Image>Adjust>Image Size*) so that it is the correct size on the page when viewed at 100%. Make the image grayscale if necessary (go to *Image>Mode>Grayscale*), and then adjust the brightness and contrast (*Image>Adjust>Brightness/Contrast*.)

❷ We want to make this image pure black and white to begin with, so set the *Contrast* to +100. A *Brightness* setting of +67 pulls the detail back out of the image, making it look like a thumbprint again rather than a black contrasty blob.

❸ Now we will make the thumbprint the color we need, rather than just black on white. Go to *Image>Mode* and choose RGB, then use *Image>Adjust>Hue/Saturation*. Click the *Colorize* checkbox, then set the *Lightness* slider to +50, and pick the *Hue* and *Saturation* settings that suit your Web page color scheme. If the *Saturation* slider is at the maximum, the image will be colorized at full strength, but this may be excessive for your needs.

78

④ Now pick *Save for Web* from the *File* menu. This shows the image in the *Save For Web* window, where you can pick from a range of useful options. First of all, click the *2-Up* tab near the top of the window to see two examples of your image. This is useful for comparing different export settings side by side.

⑤ In the *Settings* section on the right, GIF should already be selected in the top left popup menu. Below that, pick *Web* from the list of color options. This remaps any colors in the image to the ones in the Web-safe set of colors. Pick *No Dither* from the menu below that, to make sure only simple flat colors are used. Next, in the *Color Table* list below, click the little square with the background color, and then click the *Transparency* button below that panel. You should see your graphic displayed with a gray and white checkerboard pattern showing through the transparent areas.

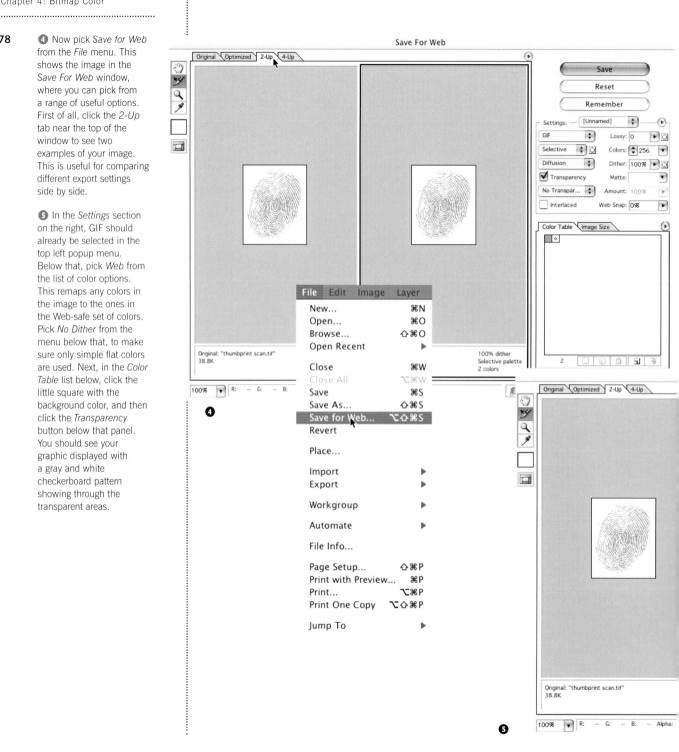

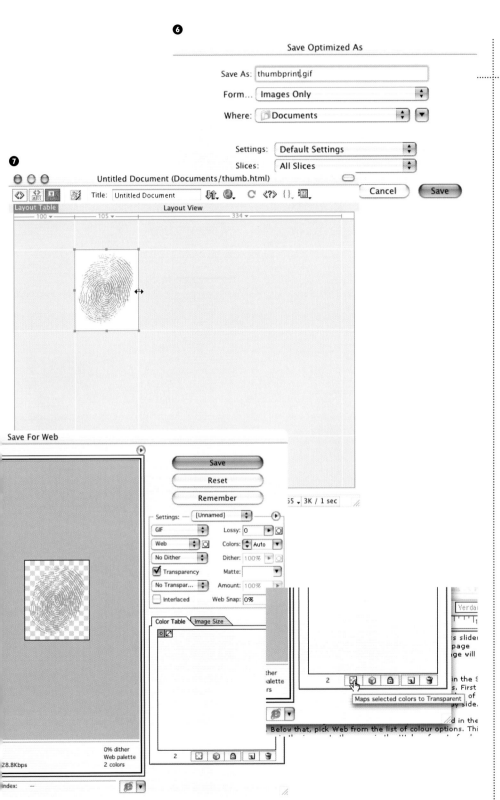

⑥ Click the *Save* button to save the graphic as a GIF image. Give it an appropriate name, leaving ".gif" at the end and remembering to use basic alphanumeric characters and no spaces. Ignore the extra options because all you need from this is the Web-ready GIF image. You should also save your Photoshop document separately, as this is your master image. You can come back to this to edit the graphic and produce more Web graphics whenever you like.

⑦ Now we can drop the finished GIF into a Web page. This is a new Dreamweaver document, with a layout cell placed on the page. The GIF file was simply dropped from the Documents folder where it was saved, straight into the cell. The cell was then resized to fit the image, and dragged into position near the left. In GoLive, you would drag an image object into a layout grid and link it to the GIF, while in Freeway you would draw an image box and import or just drop the image into place.

80 **PROJECT 12**
OPTIMIZING JPEGS

JPEG images are ideal for images with few or no sharp, high-contrast edges; graphics that use smooth graduations and soft tonal shifts; and photographic images. The JPEG compression process works on images by breaking them down into a series of tiles, and simplifying those by comparing color and contrast with nearby blocks. This process throws away image data to get file sizes down, which means that saving anything in JPEG format is a destructive process. Using a very high level of JPEG compression will result in an image with visible damage—called artefacts—particularly wherever tonal and hue changes occur. These show up as odd color fringes and blocky patches.

Even if you pick low compression settings with a JPEG file, but keep opening, editing, and resaving the image, each successive save will reapply the JPEG compression, damaging the image a little more each time. As a result, it's important to keep a master copy of any important images in a non-destructive format such as TIFF or Photoshop PSD.

❶ Open a digital photograph in an image editor such as Photoshop or Photoshop Elements. Here we have used a shot of a cloudy sky—a subject normally well-suited to the JPEG process—although any sharp divisions between cloud and sky can still pose problems.

❷ Go straight to *Save for Web* in the *File* menu, then click the *4-Up* tab. Leave the first image showing the original, then click in the second and change its settings to JPEG, high quality. Make the third JPEG medium

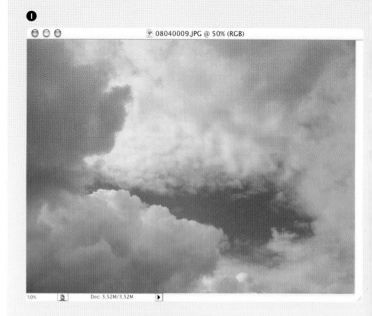

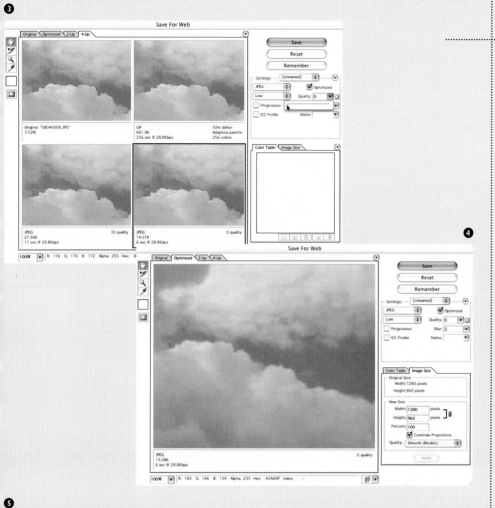

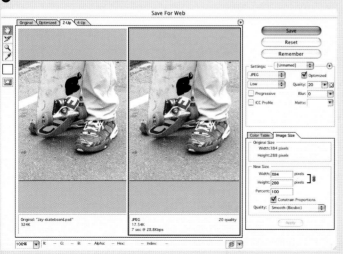

quality and the fourth JPEG low quality. The image degradation is fairly visible in the low-quality image; moderately visible (if you stop and look) in the medium-quality one; and not a problem in the high-quality one. But look at the file sizes: the low-quality image is less than a fifth of the size of the high-quality photo.

3 You can tweak the settings by using the *Quality* slider over on the right. Changing the fourth one from 10 to 0 reduces the file size even further, but the quality also drops dramatically. For comparison's sake, we have also set the top-right sample to GIF. With an adaptive palette, it actually looks pretty good, but the file size is a ridiculous 46 times larger.

4 Now to push things to the extreme, drag the *Blur* slider for the low-quality JPEG over toward the right. This applies a simple blur filter to the image, which softens all high contrast edges. Now the JPEG process can work more efficiently, so the image looks less messed up, and the file size can creep down even further. The result is not nearly as detailed as the original and still shows degradation, but it is now a tiny 13Kb image that still covers a massive 1280x960 pixel area.

5 Pick other images and see how they are handled in the *Save For Web* window. You should be able to reduce most images down to fairly small sizes without losing too much detail through judicious use of the various sliders. Watch out for color artefacts on high contrast edges, which is where they show up first.

82 PROJECT 13
OPTIMIZING PNGS

The PNG format is not very widely used, but it does offer something that GIF and JPEG don't: true 8-bit transparency, which enables areas in photographic-quality images to be given 256 different levels of transparency. JPEGs, by comparison, handle photographic images well but offer no transparency, while GIFs offer just the 1-bit "on-off" transparency, and very limited color handling.

One reason why the PNG format hasn't yet made a big impact in Web design is because older Web browsers are not able to read it. GIF and JPEG graphics can be read by virtually every browser ever made, but PNGs are restricted to the more recent versions. This shouldn't be a big cause for concern, however, as the vast majority of today's Web surfers use browsers that can cope with the format.

Another reason why PNG hasn't found great favour yet is because the file sizes are often not quite as small as GIFs or JPEGs, and the full-color PNG format (called PNG-24) doesn't offer much in the way of compression options.

Still, for the right projects, the smooth transparency option of the PNG-24 format is sheer magic, and one that, as we'll see later, opens up a range of special effects.

① **Photoshop** Take an image in Photoshop, preferably one with a transparent background, such as this fist cutout. Once the graphic is ready, choose *Save for Web* from the File menu.

② Click the *4-Up* tab, then try out the different PNG format options in a couple of the panels. PNG-24 is the JPEG alternative, and offers full 8-bit transparency, as shown here.

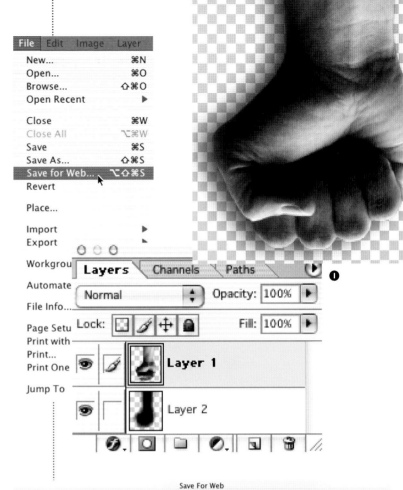

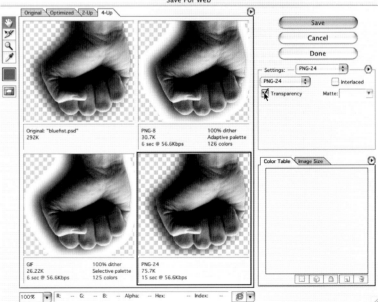

❸

❹

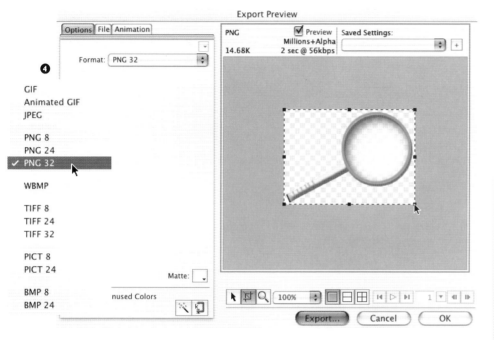

❺

This unique ability can come in very useful at times, but note that it doesn't produce particularly small file sizes. The PNG-8 option was designed as an alternative to the humble GIF, based on a reduced 256 color palette and offering a 1-bit "cutout" transparency option. However, as shown here with a file size of 30.12Kb versus 26.46Kb, it does not compress quite as well.

❸ Fireworks You may notice, when saving files from Macromedia's web graphics package, Fireworks, that it uses the PNG format for its own files. Don't try to use these files directly for websites, however, because the extra information Fireworks adds to handle all of its features means the file sizes are often more than ten times larger than an exported PNG.

❹ In Fireworks's *Export Preview* window, the options offered are PNG 8, PNG 24, and PNG 32. The PNG 24 option provides full-color support, but no transparency. If you need transparency use the PNG 32 option instead. Despite the change of name, this is exactly the same as Photoshop's PNG-24 with the transparency checkbox clicked.

❺ Dreamweaver Putting a PNG 32 graphic onto a draggable layer (see Project 7) is a good way to demonstrate the power of transparency. This magnifying glass graphic has a partially transparent lens and shadow. True, the lens does not actually magnify, but the effect is still strong. PNG Transparency enables graphics to blend in with other elements in ways that simply cannot be achieved using any other file format.

84 PROJECT 14
COLOR BACKGROUND GRAPHICS

Web pages can be given graphic image backgrounds as well as flat color backgrounds. The image is shown behind all regular page-level items, and will by default be repeated, or tiled, horizontally and vertically. This means that no matter how big the end user makes their Web page window, the background graphic will always stretch to fill it.

This behavior can be used to great effect by making a simple graphic designed to tile seamlessly. On the downside, it can be all too easy to end up with a tiled background which is so dominant that it becomes impossible to see the foreground elements or read any text.

With a little trickery, you can get around this, and also choose whether the background image is to tile in just one direction or not at all. This trick doesn't work perfectly in every Web browser around, but modern ones should be fine. Anyway, the worst that can happen is that the image will tile across and down after all.

First, we need a simple image to tile in the browser. You could simply make a rectangular selection from any graphic and save that as a Web graphic format, but the chances are that it will look very obviously tiled where the edges meet. Instead, we will make a simple, smoothly tileable image as a fake paper surface for the Web page.

❶ In Photoshop, *Copy* a square selection from a suitable image. Here we have taken a photo of a woven rug. If possible, make the selection edges sit on roughly similar parts of the pattern—as this will make life easier at the next stage. Make a note of the dimensions of the selection in the *Info* palette.

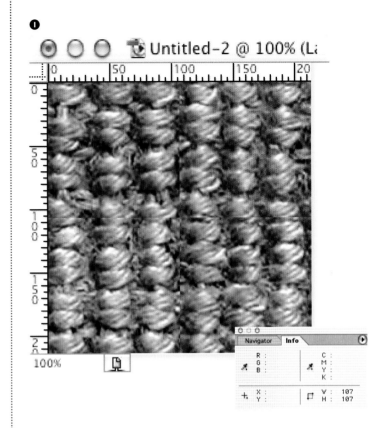

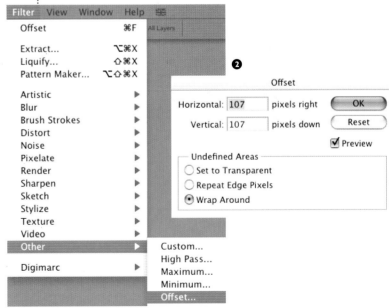

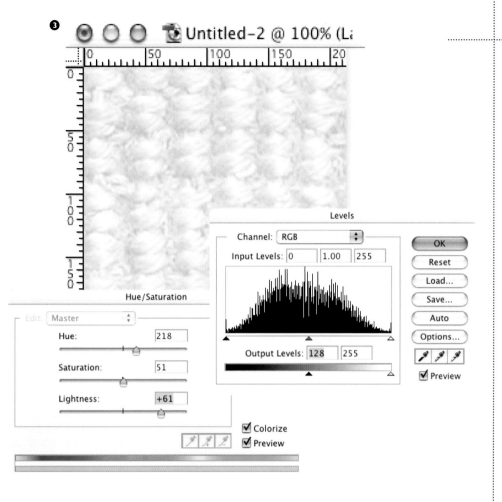

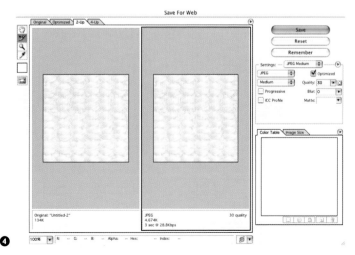

2 Make a new document window (choose *New* from the *File* menu), and *Paste* in the image. For smooth tiling, go to the *Filter* menu and slide down to *Other*, then choose *Offset*. For the horizontal and vertical offset, type in half of the image's width and height. Choose *Wrap Around*, and the result will look like this, with the problem areas running across and down the middle, and the edges now matching their opposite sides. It's now a simple matter to use the *Rubber Stamp* tool to clone small bits of the image onto the mismatched stripes.

3 Once you are done, you will have a graphic that will tile smoothly to fill any Web page window. But this is still not quite ready: it is currently far too contrasty and prominent to be suitable for a real Web page background. As it stands, any text placed on this background would be totally lost, and it is hard to imagine a color scheme into which it would fit.

To make it work, use the *Levels* or *Brightness/Contrast* controls to reduce the strength of the darker parts of the image (and possibly mute the highlights too). Now use *Hue/Saturation* to colorize, lighten, and saturate the image with an appropriate hue setting.

4 Finally, use the *Save For Web* window to pick the right compression settings. As a carefully optimized GIF, this image weighs in at a little under 20Kb; but as a JPEG with medium compression, it is less than 5Kb. Admittedly, this background is not going to set the design world alight, but it will at least give a page more texture without drawing forth any gasps of horror.

....

86

5 One of the most common uses of a tiled background graphic is not to create a full-page splash, but to make a vertical bar on the left of the page that provides a visual "shelf" for navigation buttons, sidebar text, and so on. Make a new document in Photoshop or Photoshop Elements, 1000 pixels wide by 20 pixels tall.

6 Zoom to 100% and scroll to the left. Now make a selection 200 pixels wide, from the left edge. (Choose *Rulers* from the *View* menu to help with measurements, making sure to set *Pixels* as the ruler unit type in the preferences).

7 To make color matching easier later on, switch the *Swatch* color set to Web-safe colors by picking the option from the pop-up menu in the *Swatches* palette. Choose the palest yellow available (HTML color #FFFFCC,) then choose *Fill* from the *Edit* menu to fill your selection.

8 Now choose the *Gradient* tool from the *Tools* palette, then pick the *Foreground to Transparent* gradient from the list in the toolbar. Click the black and white color chips in the *Tools* palette to reset the colors, or just press the D key. Now click to the right of the selection and drag a little way into it. This will create a gentle shadow, making it seem as if the white area is hovering above the dimmer yellow section.

9 In the *Save For Web* window, you'll find that this graphic will compress to a very small size with GIF or JPEG. As there is a sharp division and the GIF format (with adaptive palette) does not cause problems with the gradient shadow, pick the fractionally smaller GIF.

5

6

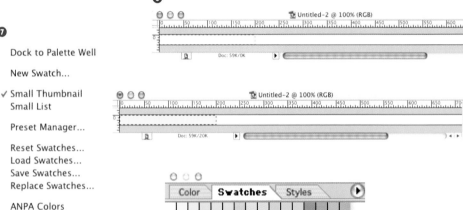

7

Dock to Palette Well

New Swatch...

✓ Small Thumbnail
  Small List

Preset Manager...

Reset Swatches...
Load Swatches...
Save Swatches...
Replace Swatches...

ANPA Colors
DIC Color Guide
FOCOLTONE Colors
HKS E
HKS K
HKS N
HKS Z
Mac OS
PANTONE metallic coated
PANTONE pastel coated
PANTONE pastel uncoated
PANTONE process coated
PANTONE solid coated
PANTONE solid matte
PANTONE solid to process
PANTONE solid uncoated
TOYO Colors
TRUMATCH Colors
VisiBone
VisiBone2
Web Hues
Web Safe Colors
Web Spectrum
Windows

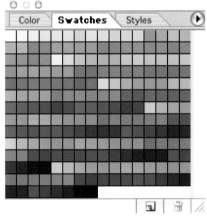

8

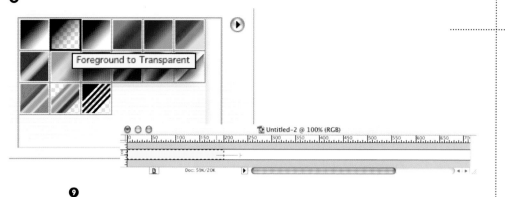

Foreground to Transparent

9

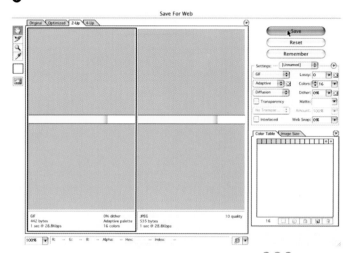

10 To see your work in action, load your Web design program and select your file as the page background. Choose *Page Properties* from the *Modify* menu in Dreamweaver. For Freeway, select *Background* from the *Page* panel in the *Inspector* palette.

11 The 200 pixel stripe on the left provides a fixed-width vertical banner that will always fill the page. (If you are able to stretch the page wider than the graphic's 1000 pixel width you will see it start to repeat, but this is generally considered wide enough for most work.)

10

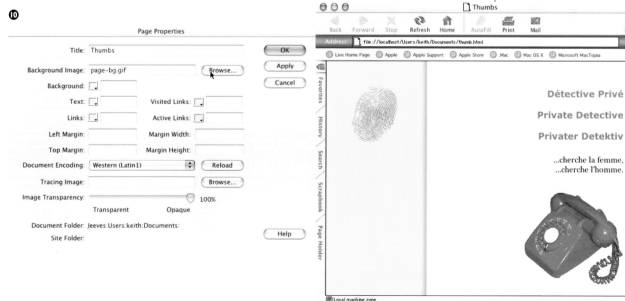

88   **PROJECT 15**

MATCHING GRAPHICS WITH BACKGROUND COLORS

Keeping an eye on the smaller details is a vital part of good Web design. This is true from the moment you place text or graphic HTML objects on a background page color or tiled image—you need to be absolutely sure that your colors match. Few things make a page layout look more unprofessional than obvious places where items of one kind have slightly different colors, or where buttons or icons have a discolored patch surrounding them.

Pseudo lighting effects, where drop shadows are cast on the page background, are another thing to watch. The default in virtually every graphics program is to have the shadow cast down and to the right, but in some cases this may not suit the overall composition of the page. If there are strongly lit photographic elements, they may even dictate the direction and strength of any shadows themselves.

Fortunately, every application used for the production of Web graphics will enable items such as drop shadows to be configured by the user. Meanwhile, pre-defined color palettes—including the standard Web-safe color palette—enable you to choose from a range of consistent colors. Keeping a note of hexadecimal color values when you select a shade can also aid you in color-matching later. Maintaining a coherent look and feel across the whole of your site takes time, but it doesn't have to be a hideous chore.

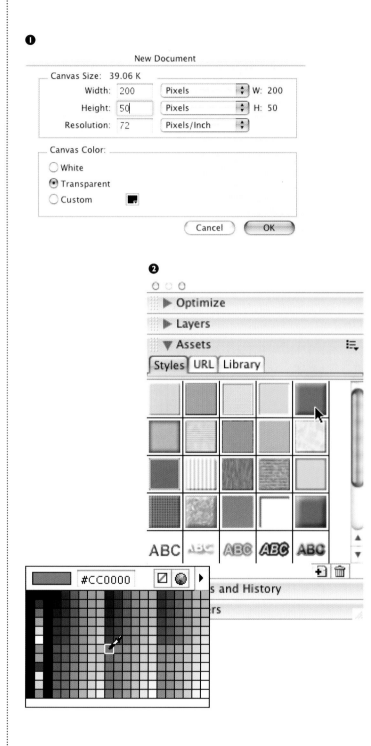

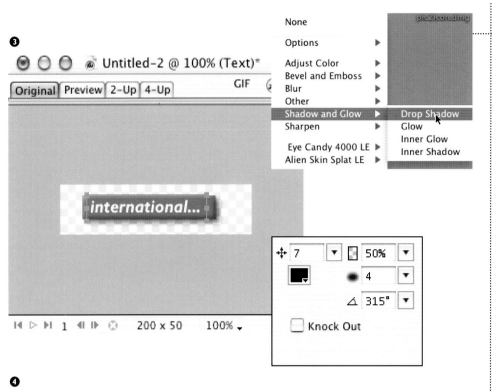

❸

❹

Export Preview

❶ Open Macromedia Fireworks and make a new document. For this example, we will make a button to fit into the 200 pixel wide vertical bar made in the previous project, so make the document 200 pixels wide and 50 pixels tall.

❷ Click the *Rectangle* tool (or press the U key) and draw out a rectangle 150 pixels wide and 24 pixels tall. Open the *Assets* palette and click the *Style 5* icon, last on the right in the first row. Now go to the *Properties* palette and change the fill color to HTML #CC0000, a dull red.

❸ Click the Effects "Plus" button in the *Properties* palette and pick *Drop Shadow* from the *Shadow and Glow* set. Set the *Transparency* to 50%. Finally, set some text on top of the button. Use a bold or heavy typeface, and make the text white so that it stands out from the deep red button.

❹ Choose *Export Preview* from the *File* menu and, in the pop-up menus, set the format to GIF and the palette to Web Adaptive. Pick *Alpha Transparency* or *Index Transparency* from the pop-up menu lower down, so that you can see the button and shadow on the checkerboard pattern.

⑤ Drop it into the Web page layout from the previous project, underneath the thumbprint graphic. You should now notice two things. First, the graphic is wider than necessary, which is a problem in Dreamweaver and GoLive because they cannot crop images themselves. Second, the drop-shadow fades out to white, while the background it sits on is pale yellow. This leaves an unpleasant white halo around the shadow.

⑥ Back in Fireworks, choose *Export Preview* again. This time, choose the right yellow (#FFFFCC) from the *Matte* pop-up color swatch. The shadow now goes from a yellow-tinged gray to the pale yellow of the background stripe. Now pick the *Crop* tool and zoom to 200%, then crop in close to the button and shadow. Click the *Export* button when you are done.

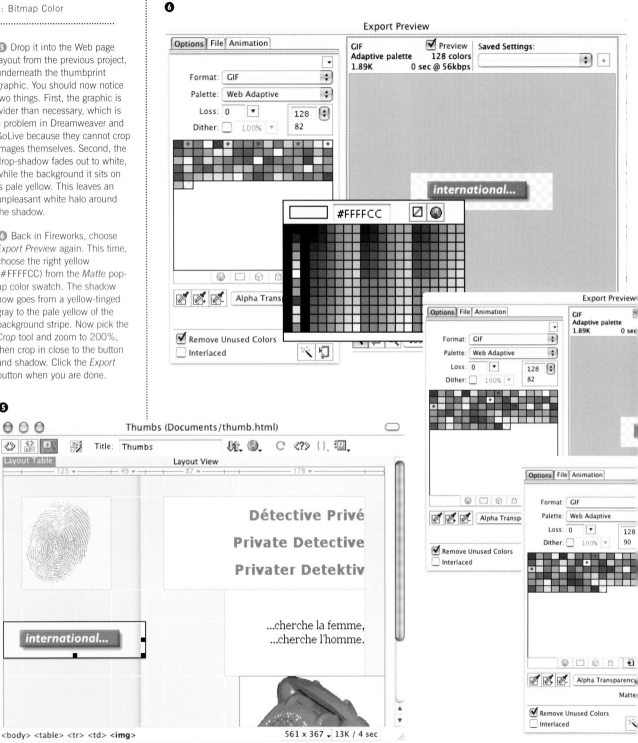

❼

❼ Go into the Web page layout and delete the existing button, then bring in the newly exported one. Now it takes only the space it needs, and blends properly with the yellow tint of the background stripe.

❽ There is only one problem left: the shadow is cast to the right, whereas the background image has a shadow cast to the left. Go back to Fireworks and select the button rectangle, then click the "i" button in the *Drop Shadow* effect line and change the degree setting to 255°. Now click on the "i" button for the *Inner Bevel* line and change the *Raised* setting to 45°.

❾ Choose *Export Preview* again. You will have to adjust the crop, or the button will be trimmed on one side. It is generally easier to do so if you zoom in to 200% first. Once done, the final button can be exported. The background and shadow match, and the light effect will not seem out of place.

❽

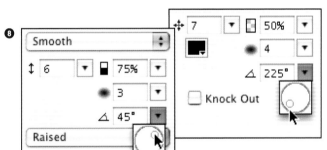

❾

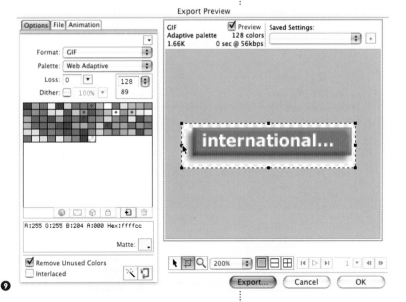

92 PROJECT 16
ADAPTING EXISTING GRAPHICS

If you are involved in professional Web design, there is a good chance that you may one day be asked to put a company logo or other ready-made graphic onto a website. Sometimes this is easy to do, but many of these graphics were never made with screen use in mind. Most of the time, you will be handed a printed letterhead, or something similar, and asked to scan from that. If you're lucky, that will be good enough, but often you will need to ask for the original artwork, preferably the computer files used to draw the logo in the first place.

One problem can be getting enough detail to show up on the screen. The kind of detail a computer display can resolve is not a patch on even a basic print. Another problem is matching color; print and screen colors often don't coincide. For example, a pure cyan, one of the standard print process colors, cannot be completely matched at all using on-screen RGB, let alone the limited Web palette. (It cuts both ways, of course, with the inability of print to match the vibrancy of a full-strength RGB red.)

If you have a clear idea of the color mix, you can often use the color mixing tools of your software to convert the CMYK print mix to the RGB color model. Sadly, this isn't the most reliable way of working, as the way a color is supposed to translate from print to screen doesn't always end up looking right when put into practice.

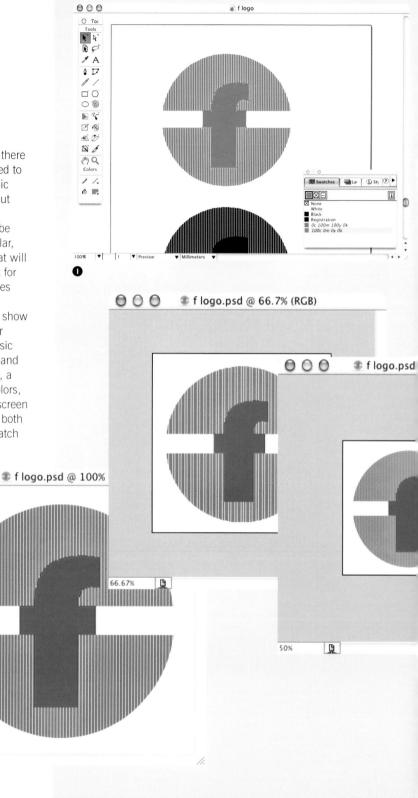

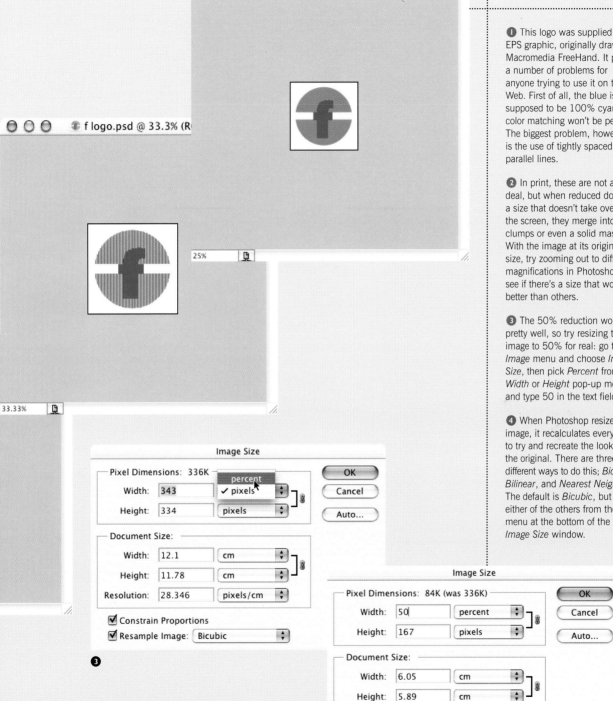

❶ This logo was supplied as an EPS graphic, originally drawn in Macromedia FreeHand. It poses a number of problems for anyone trying to use it on the Web. First of all, the blue is supposed to be 100% cyan, so color matching won't be perfect. The biggest problem, however, is the use of tightly spaced parallel lines.

❷ In print, these are not a big deal, but when reduced down to a size that doesn't take over half the screen, they merge into clumps or even a solid mass. With the image at its original size, try zooming out to different magnifications in Photoshop to see if there's a size that works better than others.

❸ The 50% reduction worked pretty well, so try resizing the image to 50% for real: go to the *Image* menu and choose *Image Size*, then pick *Percent* from the *Width* or *Height* pop-up menu and type 50 in the text field.

❹ When Photoshop resizes an image, it recalculates every pixel to try and recreate the look of the original. There are three different ways to do this; *Bicubic*, *Bilinear*, and *Nearest Neighbor*. The default is *Bicubic*, but pick either of the others from the menu at the bottom of the *Image Size* window.

94

5 Whichever method you use, you will get the best results by using clean divisions of the original size: 50%, 25%, and so on. Anything else will immediately produce more smudging and irregular patterns, as with this graphic resized to 43% using the *Nearest Neighbor* option.

6 Explaining the mechanics behind the different methods would not make for particularly interesting reading, but the results speak for themselves. *Bicubic* resampling produces the blurriest results, and while that might be good for photos, it is not usually so good for crisp line art. Here, the result is a general darkening of the red as the white lines fill in. *Bilinear* softens as well, but not nearly as much. The result is actually very close to the original logo, and is about as small as this can go without redrawing. *Nearest Neighbor* does not produce any softening at all, which may or may not produce the result you want. Here, the result is to make the red lines feel a little thin, lightening the overall effect.

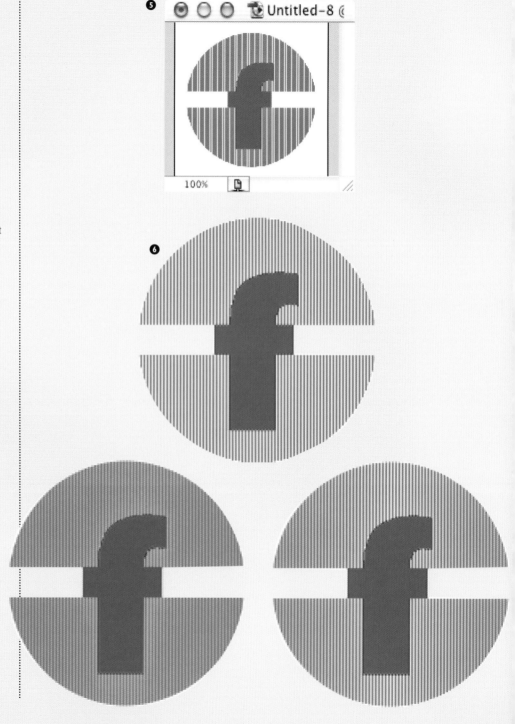

❼ Unsharp Mask

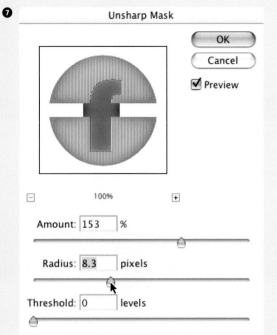

OK
Cancel
☑ Preview

100%

Amount: 153 %

Radius: 8.3 pixels

Threshold: 0 levels

❼ Applying the *Unsharp Mask* filter to the *Bicubic* resampled image can help pull back some of the definition, but there is always a price to pay for this sort of to-and-fro work with images. As soon as you push the amount high enough to make an appreciable difference, the edges of the lines start to join together. This can be exaggerated by pushing up the *Radius* level to make the sharpening process affect broader areas. But unless you are actually redesigning the graphic, that's not a good idea.

❽ The 50% scale with the *Bilinear* resampling produced the most useful result before editing. However, if a smaller image is to be used, some manual work on the original image is necessary—without this, the red lines turn into a solid mass. What is needed is some basic thinning out of the lines, because they blend together as the logo shrinks. Use the *Magic Wand* tool to select and delete every other line.

❾ Now when the graphic is resized to 25% (using *Bicubic* resampling), the lines don't blend together too much. The red lines are, in fact, a little lighter than those in the original. Some careful work with layers could improve this to an extent, but that sort of thing is normal when dealing with small graphics at screen resolution.

❽
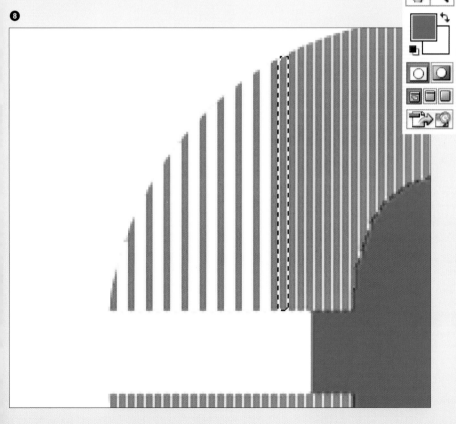

❾

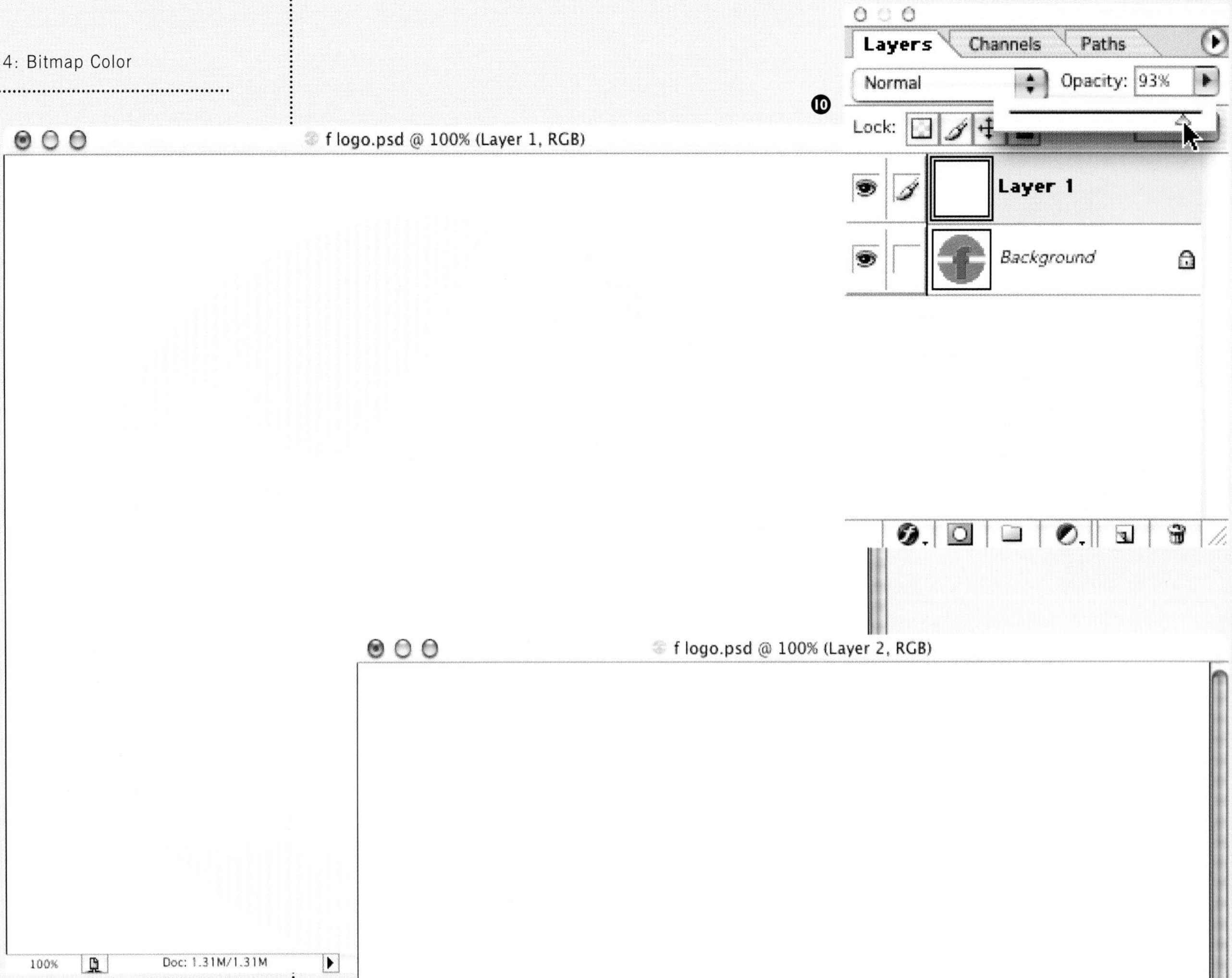

f logo.psd @ 100% (Layer 1, RGB)

Layers \ Channels \ Paths

Normal ⟂ Opacity: 93% ▶

❿

Lock: ☐ ✐ ✛

👁 🖌 **Layer 1**

👁 *Background* 🔒

f logo.psd @ 100% (Layer 2, RGB)

100% Doc: 1.31M/1.31M ▶

❿ Another way to use logos, particularly troublesome ones, is as large but subtle page "watermark" images. Use *Image Size* in the *Image* menu to scale the image up so it is big enough to fill the Web page you're designing. This is enlarged by 200%. Then add a layer, fill it with white, and make it slightly less than 100% opaque. The image should now show through faintly as a colored tint of its former self.

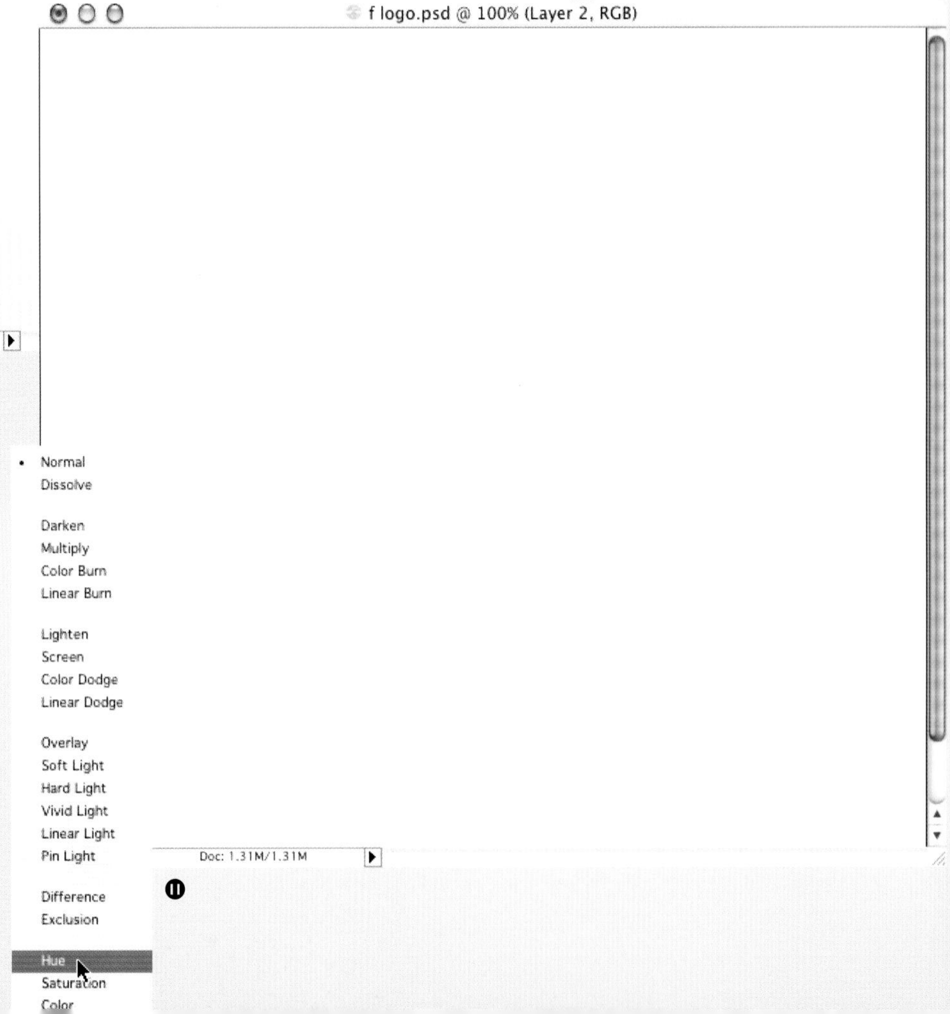

- Normal
  Dissolve

  Darken
  Multiply
  Color Burn
  Linear Burn

  Lighten
  Screen
  Color Dodge
  Linear Dodge

  Overlay
  Soft Light
  Hard Light
  Vivid Light
  Linear Light
  Pin Light

  Difference
  Exclusion

  Hue
  Saturation
  Color

Doc: 1.31M/1.31M ▶

⓫

⑫

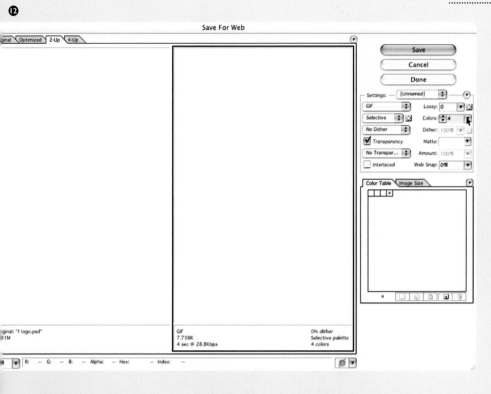

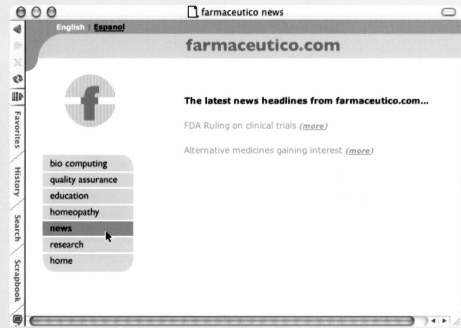

⑪ Add another layer and fill this with white as well. Then set the *Light* mode pop-up menu in the *Layers* palette to *Hue*, which applies this layer's hue to the ones underneath. And as white (or gray or black for that matter) has no hue, this also changes the image beneath to monochrome. Move the *Opacity* slider to 60% to enable a hint of the original color— already washed out by the transparent white layer—to show through.

⑫ Save this image, then use it as a page background image. The result looks like a watermark-style graphic printed on white paper. The small graphic can be used in a more conventional manner, but watch out for the edges. This has been saved as a transparent GIF to help blend it into the page, but the antialiased edges, where pixels were blended during resampling, give a white halo around the colors. On a pale background, this won't be noticed. However, if used against a darker background, the image would have to be made again, matted to the appropriate colors.

98 PROJECT 17
ADVANCED JPEG COMPRESSION

Because the JPEG compression process prefers soft images with little or no areas of high contrast, you will often get smaller file sizes if you simply blur your graphics before saving. The downside, of course, is that you end up with soft, detail-free results. One solution is to use selective blurring to soften the background in an image but leave the area of interest nice and sharp. This requires a little work, but when done with care, the results should work well and can even enhance the impact of the image. Often the end viewer will not even notice the trick you've pulled, and their attention will be focused on the item left unblurred. This will let you get graphics down to smaller sizes without having to use more image-damaging levels of compression. Less artefacting, less chance of rogue color contamination, and smaller files—precisely what every Web designer wants.

A similar approach is to cut the item out altogether, and place it on a flat color background. You can then force every image to conform to a site-wide color scheme, where either the whole graphic stands from the rest of the page background or where each JPEG mattes in as a pseudo cutout.

❶ If you are building a composite image, the blurring process is easy: keep the item of interest on its own layer and blur the layers beneath.

❷ You can also use *Hue/Saturation* changes to pull the foreground item out of the composition, as in this example. Although the fist has sharp edges, most of the background has been softened.

❸ With the JPEG quality setting at medium, this image takes just over 7Kb. If the blur had been applied to the sharp

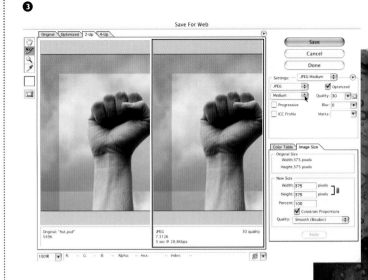

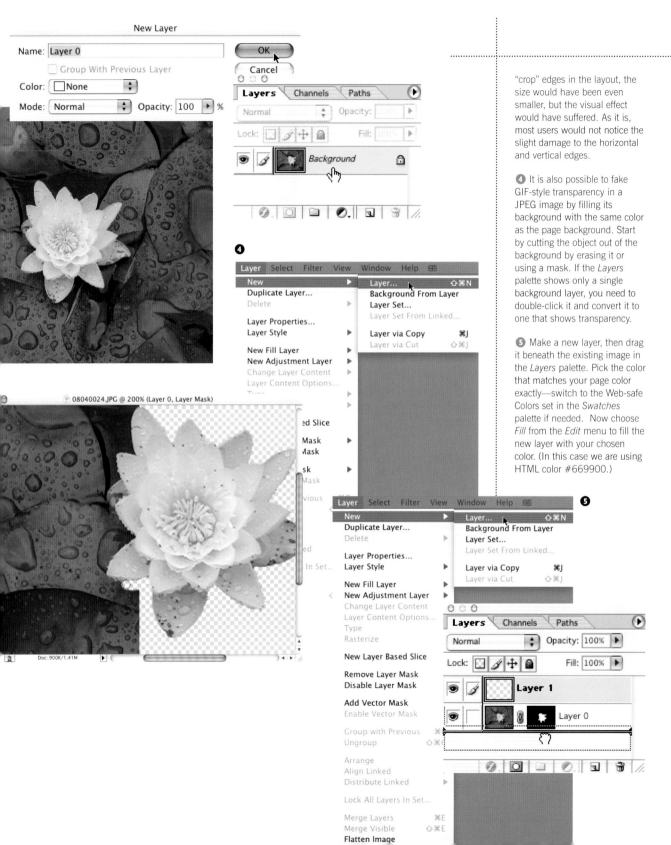

"crop" edges in the layout, the size would have been even smaller, but the visual effect would have suffered. As it is, most users would not notice the slight damage to the horizontal and vertical edges.

❹ It is also possible to fake GIF-style transparency in a JPEG image by filling its background with the same color as the page background. Start by cutting the object out of the background by erasing it or using a mask. If the *Layers* palette shows only a single background layer, you need to double-click it and convert it to one that shows transparency.

❺ Make a new layer, then drag it beneath the existing image in the *Layers* palette. Pick the color that matches your page color exactly—switch to the Web-safe Colors set in the *Swatches* palette if needed. Now choose *Fill* from the *Edit* menu to fill the new layer with your chosen color. (In this case we are using HTML color #669900.)

100

❻ If you have specified the page background color in the Web design program using HTML color codes, then there is a chance that the color you used in the image may not match the page when viewed in some Web browsers. This problem shows in some Web browsers when the screen is set to 16-bit color (also known as "thousands of colors" on Macs, and "High Color" on Windows).

❼ To get around this, use a small snippet of the background from your graphic to make a one-color tile for use as a page background. Make a small selection—say, a 50 pixel square—and *Copy* it, then make a new document and *Paste*.

❽ Choose *Save for Web* from the *File* menu and use the same settings as for the main graphic. If you use a different format, the colors will probably still not quite match, and big differences in compression settings (even with the same format) can also cause color shifts.Return to your Web design program and use the exported graphic for the page background graphic. This will help the problem, although in some cases the foreground image will still appear slightly different. If this is a persistent problem, consider making your images as transparent GIFs or transparent PNGs.

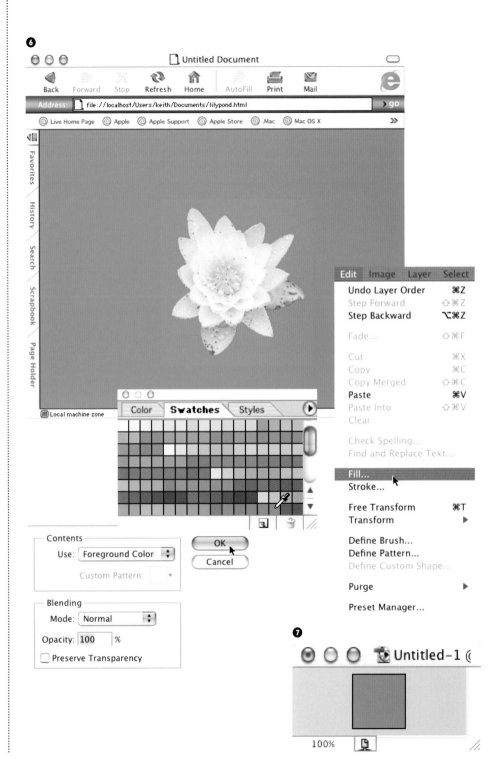

8

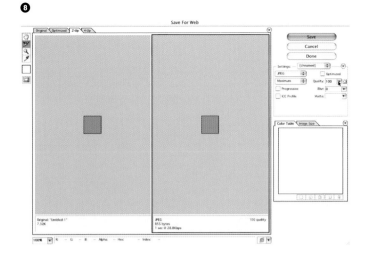

9 You can use the background color to help blend graphics into the background in other ways as well. Here, water drops are being copied from this photo. The *Magic Wand* selection tool makes selecting shapes relatively simple; just click, and similar areas will be selected. Hold down the Shift key and click to add to the selection, and hold down Alt (Option) to take away from the current selection.

9

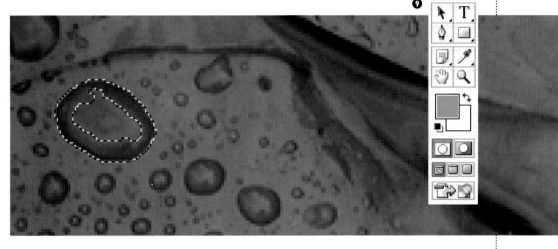

10

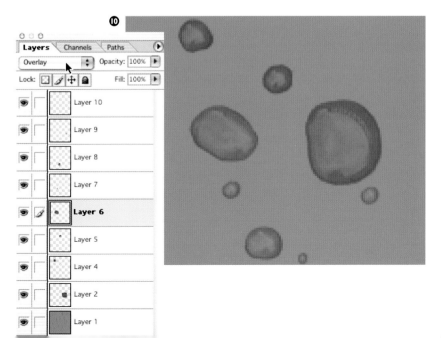

10 *Copy*, then *Paste* your selection into the image with the background color. Whatever you *Paste* is placed on a new layer. Hold down the Apple key (if you're using a Mac) or the Control key (if you're using Windows) and click an object. That selects its layer. Now click the *Normal* pop-up menu in the *Layers* palette and pick *Overlay*. The image will now blend smoothly with the background color, with only the value (the lightness of the image) showing. The color is now completely set by the underlying image.

102 PROJECT 18
OPTIMIZING IMAGES
WITHIN LAYOUTS

The process of optimizing images as GIFs or JPEGs can end up causing some color changes. These can be minimal, but if you try to get your image file sizes down as much as possible, you can end up with graphics that don't quite work in carefully crafted layouts. The best way to be sure your images will work completely smoothly on the page is to optimize them from within the actual layouts. You can step back and forth between optimizing and page layout tools to check things in Dreamweaver and GoLive, but this is not the simplest of methods. Rather than relying on extra software, Freeway can handle producing optimized Web graphics itself, and this is easily done right on the page. Other advantages come with this, not the least being easy cropping, scaling, and rotating, and support for almost any graphic file format. As the final Web graphics can be produced within the layout environment, you can collage different elements together on the page, both images and graphic text, and have a single Web graphic produced from the result. The only problem is that the software is Mac-only; Windows users will just have to carry on switching between programs.

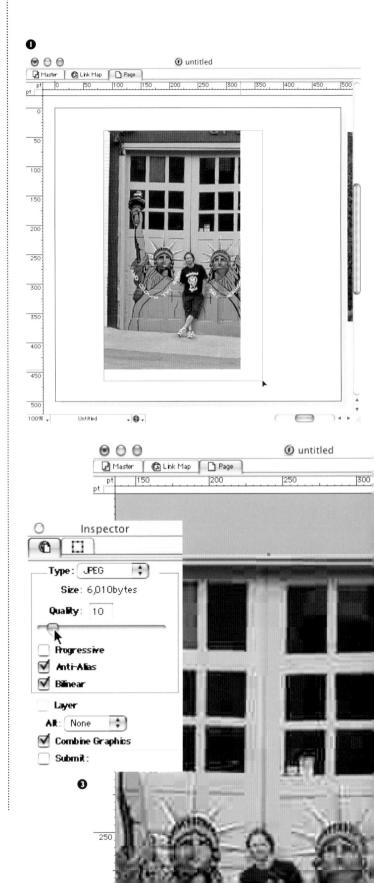

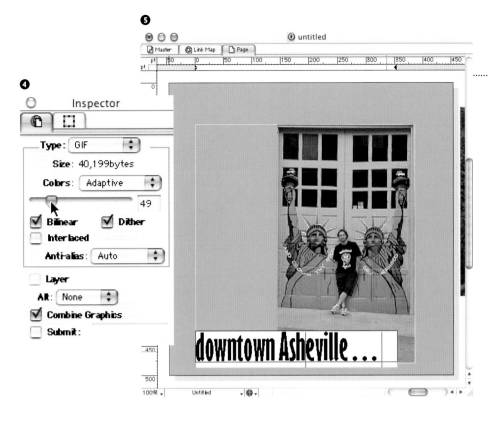

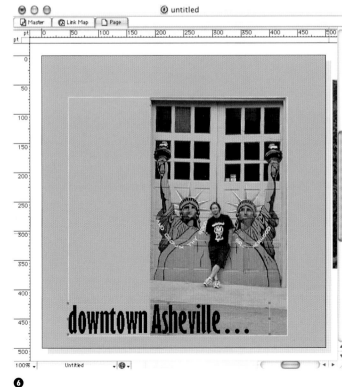

① Graphics in Freeway are placed in graphic boxes, drawn on the page using the *Sketch Graphic Item* or *Pen* tools. Once a box is made, you can *Import* images from the *File* menu, or drag them from any graphics program or the Finder. You can also crop the image, pan it around in the box, and scale it up and down.

② To see how an image is to be optimized, choose *View>Graphics Preview*. All graphics are rendered using their current format and quality settings and shown as they would be exported. To change the settings, click on an image, then click the first tab in the *Inspector* palette.

③ Pick JPEG from the *Type* menu if it isn't already selected, and try moving the *Quality* slider to the left. When you let go, the image is updated using the new compression level, and you can see if there is any discrepancy caused between it and the background color or graphics.

④ Try the other formats, playing with the sliders to adjust the appearance, and comparing the graphic's byte size shown in the *Inspector* palette each time.

⑤ Now draw another graphic box on top of the first one. Click inside and type a title. This is graphic text; any typeface you have installed can be used, and the final result is rendered as a bitmap. Select the text and choose a font and size from the *Style* menu or *Inspector* palette.

⑥ If *Outlines* is selected in the *View* menu, you will see a bounding box outline surrounding both graphic shapes; this is the extent of the composite Web graphic that will be made from the two elements.

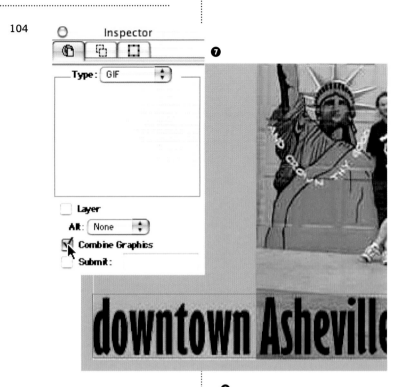

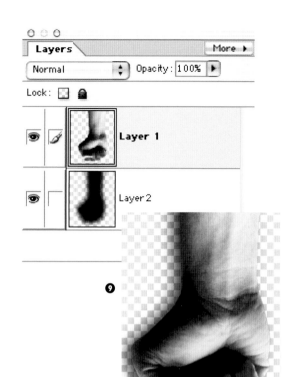

❼ If you have heavy JPEG compression applied, the *Graphic Preview* option will show how this damages the shape of the text graphic. To counter this, you can reduce the compression level of the first object, or you can turn off the *Combine Graphics* option in the *Inspector* palette's first tab.

❽ This produces sliced graphics in the final output, with different settings applied to each element. This can lead to color changes in different parts, so watch for this. Turn on *HTML Preview* in the *View* menu to see exactly how the items will be sliced up.

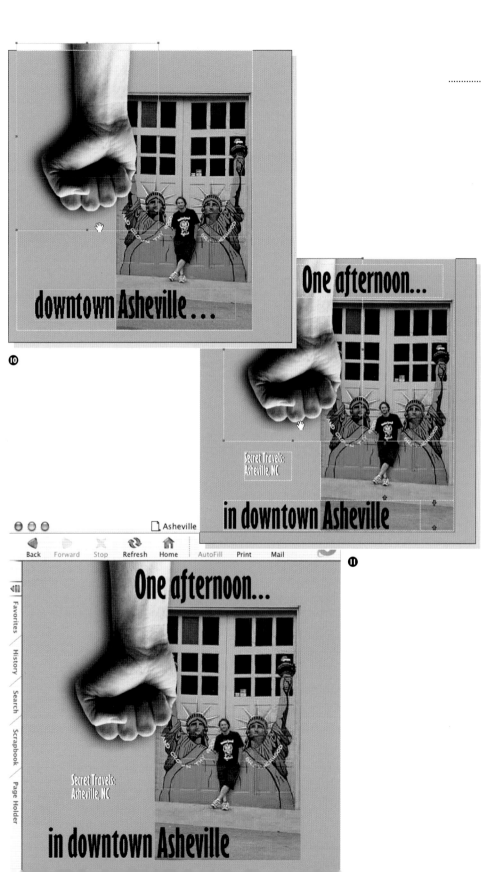

9 You can import many different graphic file formats, including TIFF, EPS, PNG, and native Photoshop and Illustrator files. To see how much can be done with in-layout composition, make an image in Photoshop with transparent areas (Photoshop Elements is equally good for this). If you have trouble with this, just make a new layer and delete the first, using the *Layers* palette. When you have an image with soft transparent areas, save it as a regular Photoshop file (.psd).

10 Now bring the image into a graphic box in Freeway. Drag the box over other items and you will see the transparency in action. You may find that turning off *Graphics Preview* until you want to check the optimizing is a good move, as this slows things down with lots of graphic boxes on the page.

11 What you get in the end result is a combined Web-ready graphic with the visual appearance of your multiple-object layout. Best of all, you can adjust the collage and edit the graphic text at any time. This proves very useful if you are perfecting a graphic-heavy layout for a choosy client.

106 **PROJECT 19**
COLOR GIFS AND TRANSPARENCY

Not all images are easy to make transparent, and if you have a product shot that you want to use as a cutout, you need to handle things slightly differently. You may have the luxury of images shot in a studio, or you may have to make do with digital snaps taken in the office or home, but wherever the photos come from, you will probably have to cut things away from the background.

Teaming the different selection tools up with the *QuickMask* makes this task much easier. These two methods of making selection are radically different, but you can shift between them very easily.

❷

Dock to Palette Well

New Channel...
Duplicate Channel...
Delete Channel

New Spot Channel...
Merge Spot Channel

Quick Mask Options...

Split Channels
Merge Channels...

Palette Options...

Color Picker

Select Quick Mask color:

OK
Cancel
Custom

○ H: 200 ° ○ L: 66
○ S: 100 % ○ a: -14
○ B: 100 % ○ b: -53

○ R: 0   C: 67 %
○ G: 170 M: 22 %
○ B: 255 Y: 0 %
00AAFF K: 0 %

☐ Only Web Colors

❶

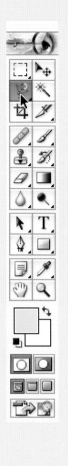

❶ On the surface this image looks quite simple to work with, but the curly cable and the shadow from the flash mean that it still needs to be handled with some care.

❷ To separate the phone from the background, we are going to use the *QuickMask*, a special masking method which lets you paint over areas to be hidden. By default, Photoshop shows this mask as a red overlay—but as the phone itself is red, this could make it hard to tell the mask and the image apart. We can change the color of the *QuickMask* by selecting *QuickMask Options* from the *Tool Options* pop-up in the *Channels* palette. Use a blue mask in this case.

❸ The *Magnetic Lasso* tool in Photoshop or Photoshop Elements is ideal for the first stage of the cutting-out process. Just draw around the edge of the item with this selection tool and a roughly accurate selection will be made. Click to add "anchor points" if the selection seems to be getting out of hand.

❹ Now click the *QuickMask* button in the *Tools* palette, and your selection will be converted to a mask channel, appearing as a transparent blue layer on top of the photograph. Pick the *Brush* tool, choosing a small brush (the 5 pixel hard round brush is a good size), then zoom in on the image and start painting in the flaws in the red mask. Paint with black to fill in holes in the blue mask, and paint with white to erase parts of the mask.

108

❺ Click the *Standard Mode* button to turn the *QuickMask* into a selection. As you have put so much effort into making this mask, it is worth saving it in case you want to use it again. Choose *Save Selection* from the *Selection* menu, and give it a logical name. Then choose *Copy* from the *Edit* menu and make a new document. Finally, *Paste* what you have just copied into this new window.

❻ Next, scale the image to the size you want it to be on the Web page. Choose *Image Size* from the *Image* menu, and type in the pixel width or height that you want. This image is to be 200 pixels wide; a little less than a third of the original size. If the image now looks a little soft, go to the *Filters* menu and use one of the *Sharpen* filters.

❼ The next step is to clean up the soft edges of the cutout, as they will have pale fringing which will show up on many backgrounds. Choose *Load Selection* from the *Selection* menu and click *OK*. Now click on the *QuickMask* button once more, then use the *Brightness/Contrast* adjustment with *Brightness* at -100 and *Contrast* at +100. Turn this back to a selection and use to trim off any semi-transparent pixels and give the cutout a hard edge.

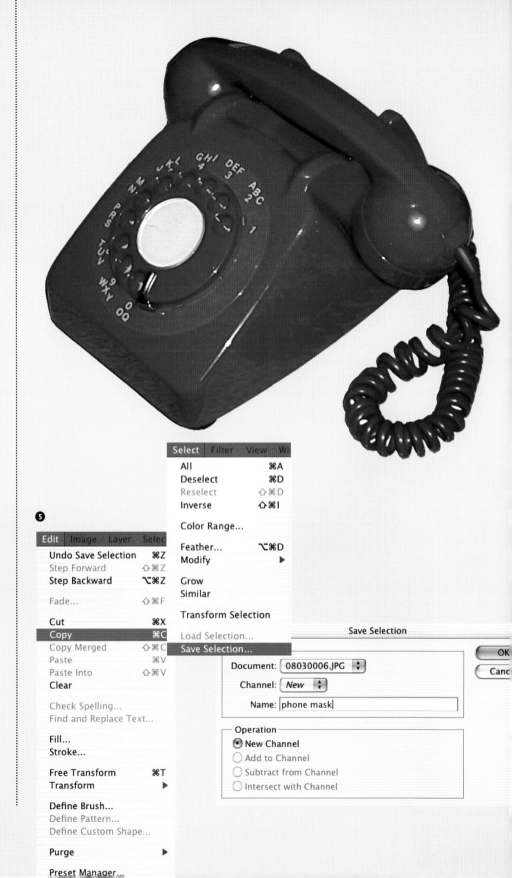

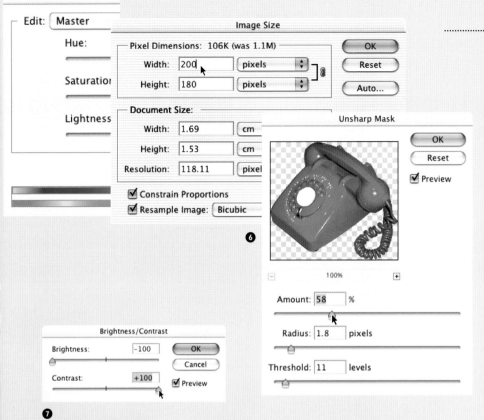

Edit: Master

Hue:

Saturation

Lightness

Image Size

Pixel Dimensions: 106K (was 1.1M)

Width: 200 pixels

Height: 180 pixels

OK
Reset
Auto...

Document Size:

Width: 1.69 cm

Height: 1.53 cm

Resolution: 118.11 pixel

☑ Constrain Proportions
☑ Resample Image: Bicubic

❻

Unsharp Mask

OK
Reset
☑ Preview

– 100% +

Amount: 58 %

Radius: 1.8 pixels

Threshold: 11 levels

❽ Pick *Save for Web* from the *File* menu, and click the *2-Up* tab. The image probably looks either very pixellated or patchy. One solution is to play with the *Dither* settings. The other is to pick *Adaptive* from the second menu on the left; this uses the most appropriate set of colors rather than the limited set of reds in the Web-safe palette. With this option, you can pick 32 or even 16 colors from the *Colors* popup menu, reducing the file size to less than half that of the 256-color GIF.

Brightness/Contrast

Brightness: –100

Contrast: +100

OK
Cancel
☑ Preview

❼

Select | Filter | View | Wi

All ⌘A
Deselect ⌘D
Reselect ⇧⌘D
Inverse ⇧⌘I

Color Range...

Feather... ⌥⌘D
Modify ▶

Grow
Similar

Transform Selection

Load Selection...
Save Selection...

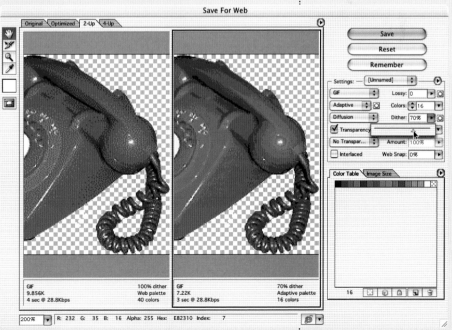

Save For Web

Original | Optimized | 2-Up | 4-Up

Save
Reset
Remember

Settings: [Unnamed]

GIF Lossy: 0

Adaptive Colors: 16

Diffusion Dither: 70%

☑ Transparency

No Transpar... Amount: 100%

☐ Interlaced Web Snap: 0%

Color Table | Image Size

GIF
9.856K
4 sec @ 28.8Kbps
100% dither
Web palette
40 colors

GIF
7.22K
3 sec @ 28.8Kbps
70% dither
Adaptive palette
16 colors

16

❽

200% R: 232 G: 35 B: 16 Alpha: 255 Hex: E82310 Index: 7

110 PROJECT 20
ANTIALIASING EDGES

Dealing with images meant for use on screen means working with relatively chunky pixels, much larger than anything print designers would ever touch. Without help, curves and diagonal lines will always look a bit rough, as the individual pixels form a jagged staircase effect. The way graphics programs get around this is to use a blurring trick called antialiasing. In a nutshell, this involves taking pixels along the problem edges and blending them with the adjacent color. Ironically, by softening the otherwise sharp and ragged edges, this process actually makes images look much sharper. Antialiasing is generally done automatically by the graphics program, coming into play—for instance—when creating graphic type.

When dealing with transparent GIF images, the issue of antialiasing can make things rather complex. As GIF transparency is a simple on/off setting, it doesn't tend to work well with antialiased edges (or not without some planning, at least.) If a graphic is antialiased against a white background, then made transparent and shown on a dark Web page, the blended edges will appear as a pale halo, which is going to look ugly on screen. The trick is to know what color the Web page will be, and to antialias against that in the graphics program. When a page background has a number of different colors, pick the one that is most dominant.

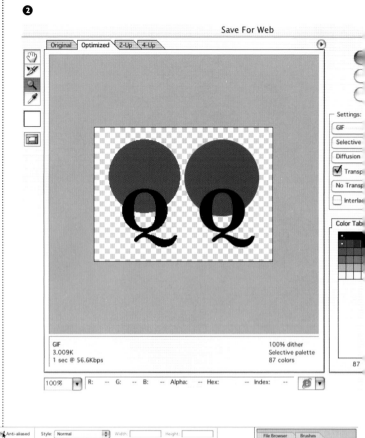

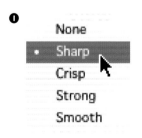

None
· Sharp
Crisp
Strong
Smooth

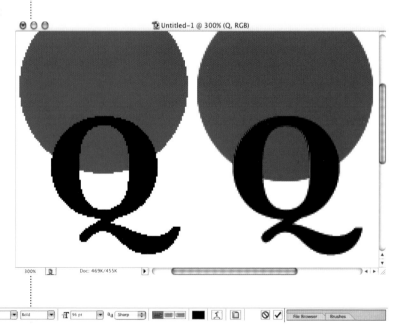

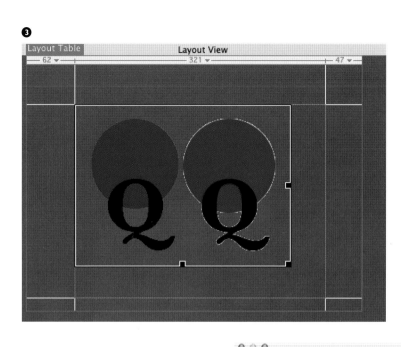

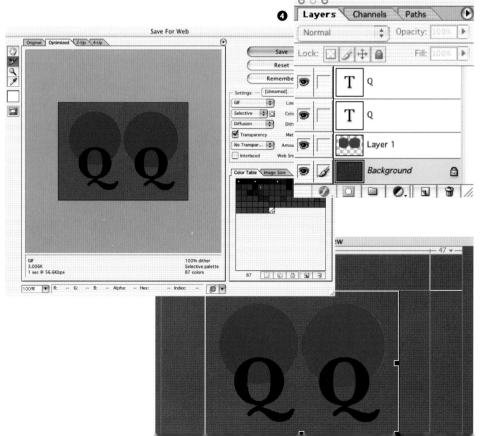

❶ Photoshop Photoshop (and Photoshop Elements) offer three different antialias settings for type, plus the option of turning off antialiasing for selection tools. Make two separate type layers, each with a large, curvy character. Using the *Options* bar by the menu bar, set the antialiasing of one to *None*. Now draw a couple of ellipses with the *Ellipse* selection tool, turning off antialiasing for one before you make it. Fill each one with a color as you go, then zoom in and spot the difference.

❷ Choose *Save for Web* from the *File* menu and set the format to GIF, making sure that transparency is switched on. It all looks fine here, but the acid test is when the transparent GIF is used on a page.

❸ Here the GIF has been placed onto a Dreamweaver page that has been given a dark background color. You will rapidly see how antialiasing, when made using the wrong "background" color, can be much worse than none at all.

❹ Go back to Photoshop and fill the background layer with an appropriate shade, then choose *Save for Web* again. Choose the eyedropper tool and click the gray, then finally click the small *Map Transparency* button in the lower-right of the window. Now that the image has the right background and knows that it is to be transparent, the antialiasing and cutout will work well with the Web page background. Note that you will need to remake the image if the background color changes.

112

5 Fireworks Fireworks is rather more flexible about the antialiasing of graphics, largely because it treats each shape as a separate object rather than a mass of bitmap brush strokes. Pick the *Ellipse* tool and draw a circle. The default setting is antialiased, but you can change this at any time. Make three shapes, then use the *Properties* palette to try out the different settings. Zoom in to see things in detail.

6 Fireworks' type control is equally flexible. Set some text, make it fairly large, and try out the antialias settings in the *Properties* palette. The *No Anti-Alias* option turns off all smoothing, but the differences between the other three options are more subtle.

7 With very thin type such as this, duplicating a text box will increase the strength of the lines. This works because the semi-transparent antialiased edges add up to more opaque pixels. The effect becomes crude and pixelated if you add too many copies however, because all the antialiasing ends up solid, and the shape's edge is once more just hard pixels.

8 Choose *Export Preview* from the *File* menu, and make sure the format is set to GIF and a transparency option is selected below. Just as with Photoshop, the antialias "blurring" should be done using an appropriate background color. However, rather than play around with filling the background in the main document, just pick the appropriate hue from the *Matte* pop-up color picker.

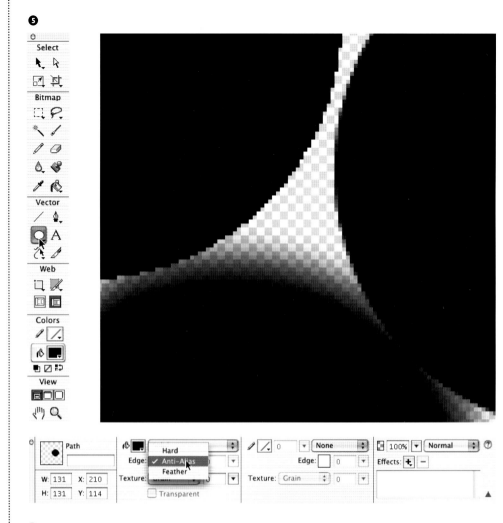

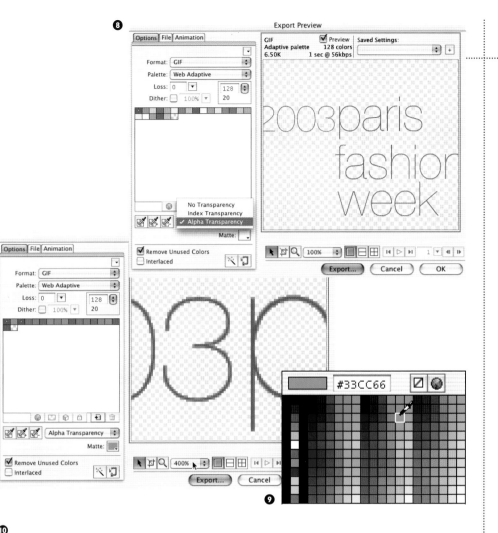

9 The results are shown immediately in the *Export Preview* window. Pick the color that comes closest to the Web page background, and any antialiased shapes will be surrounded with a sharp-edged halo of that color. Zoom in on the preview to see how it works.

10 As shown here in GoLive, when the graphic is placed in a Web page with the right background color (or a background image that is largely the right color), the color halo mattes invisibly with the rest of the page, leaving you with a beautifully antialiased graphic that sits very comfortably within the layout.

11 Freeway The "antialias to" concept of choosing a color to use for blending is found in other programs too. For example, Freeway offers an antialias pop-up menu for graphics. The Auto option is almost always fine, but other colors can be chosen manually, or antialiasing can be turned off altogether. With *Graphics Preview* turned on, it is easy to see the effects of a wrong manual antialias color choice.

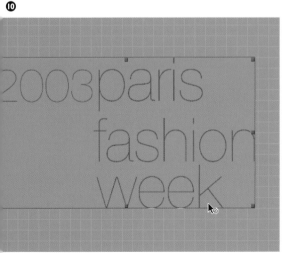

114 PROJECT 21
BACKGROUND GRAPHIC EFFECTS

Normally, images used as page backgrounds tile across the page and scroll along with everything else. This is usually exactly what is wanted, but sometimes it can be nice to exert a little more control. Forcing a page background image to tile in only one direction—either horizontally or vertically, but not both—is possible with a little JavaScript. Another closely related trick, which can come in very useful from time to time, is to prevent the background image from scrolling, while leaving the regular page elements—the text and foreground graphics—to scroll as normal.

This particular set of tricks isn't documented particularly well in any of the three website design programs, but it is all quite possible to achieve with a little care. With a little forethought about the background and foreground colors—and, of course, the antialiasing—the results can be stunning.

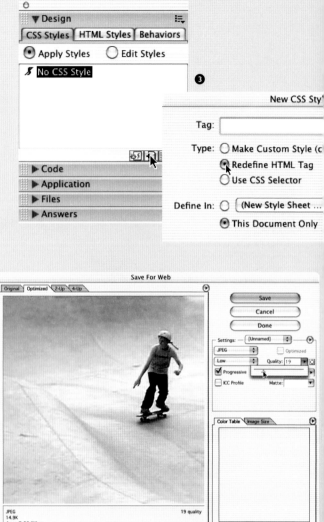

❹

New CSS Style

OK

Cancel

Tag: body

○ OK

Tag: body

Type: ○ Make Custom Style (class)
◉ Redefine HTML Tag
○ Use CSS Selector

Define In: ○ (New Style Sheet ...)
◉ This Document Only

OK

Cancel

Help

a
abbr
acronym
address
applet
area
b
base
basefont
bdo
big
blockquote
✓ body
br
button
caption
center
cite
code
col
colgroup
dd
del
dfn
dir
div
dl
dt
em
fieldset
font
form
▼

CSS Style definition for body

Category

Type
Background
Block
Box
Border
List
Positioning
Extensions

Background

Background Color:

Background Image: file:///Malcom/Users/keith/[Browse...

Repeat:

Attachment:
    scroll
    fixed

Horizontal Position:

Vertical Position: pixels

Help   Apply Cancel OK

❺

❶ First of all, use Photoshop to prepare the picture you want to use as the background image. This graphic is designed to cover most of the height of an average Web page, fading out to white as it nears the bottom of its 596 pixel height. It is also 1,280 pixels across, broad enough to cover the full width of all but the most unreasonably wide browser windows.

❷ Export the image as a Web graphic, choosing the heaviest compression settings for which the image will work without looking bad. In this case, we have saved as a JPEG in Photoshop's Low quality setting. The background blur trick shown in Project 8 was used to soften parts of the image a little, which also helps to keep the file size slim.

❸ **Dreamweaver** If you are working in Dreamweaver, go to the *CSS Styles* pane (in the *Design* palette; choose *CSS Styles* from the *Window* menu if necessary), and click the *New Style* button.

❹ Pick *Redefine HTML Tag* from the *New CSS Style* window, and choose *Body* from the pop-up *Tag* list. Click *OK* and the *CSS Style Definition* window will open.

❺ Click *Background* in the *Category* list, then click the *Browse* button and pick a background image. Now pick *Fixed* from the *Attachment* pop-up menu. If you want to prevent image tiling in the browser window, click the *Repeat* pop-up menu and choose *No-Repeat* (or *Repeat-X* or *-Y* for tiling in just one direction).

116

6 Lay out the rest of the page, being sure to plan the antialias matting color for any transparent GIFs carefully. As things will move across the background image, edges might not look perfect when moving over all parts of the background. Now preview the result in a Web browser. (Press the F12 key to step to the default browser.) When the page is scrolled, the background image will stay put while the text and graphics in the foreground move freely.

7 GoLive Performing this trick in GoLive involves a little more fiddling, but nothing too complex. Pull down the *View* menu and choose *CSS Editor*. In the *CSS Editor* window, click the pop-up menu button in the top-right corner, then slide to *New Style* and pick *Body*.

7

8

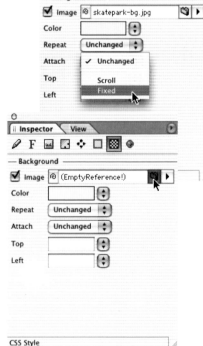

6

Over 17,000 square feet of skateable surface

Three distinct areas:

* **Beginner's Bowl**
* **Intermediate to advanced Street Course**
* **Deep Bowl for advanced skaters**

Asheville's Food Lion Skatepark is the premier skateboard facility in North Carolina and the surrounding states!

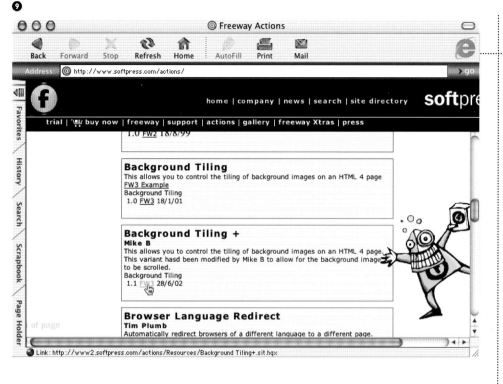

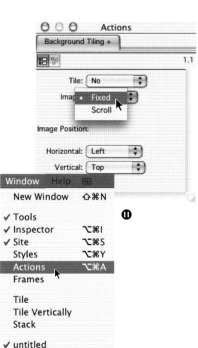

8 Next, move across to the *Inspector* palette, which now shows the *Background* settings. Click the *Image* checkbox, then click the folder button and pick your background image. Once this is done, choose *Fixed* from the *Attach* pop-up menu. If you want to control the repeat tiling, use the *Repeat* menu, which can be found immediately above the *Attach* menu.

9 **Freeway** Freeway requires an "Action" for this trick: go to www.softpress.com/actions and click the *Actions Library* link, then the A-E link. Download one of the *Background Tiling* Actions, unstuff it, and drop into the Freeway *Actions* folder.

10 In the Freeway layout, add the background image by using the *Inspector* palette's *Image* pop-up. Now apply the newly installed *Background Tiling* action by picking it from the *Actions* list in the *Page* menu.

11 To configure the action, choose *Actions* from the *Window* menu, then make your settings in the *Actions* palette. Set the *Image* to be *Fixed*, and pick your preferred *Tile* settings. Whichever website design program you use, this trick can give your page a radically different look and feel.

118 **PROJECT 22**
GIF TEXT

Text in Web pages can be made in one of two ways: as formatted HTML, or as a graphic. There are advantages and disadvantages to both approaches. HTML text prints cleanly, it can be copied and pasted directly from the Web browser, and it can reflow to fit the page width. For people with modem-based Internet connections, it is also generally much faster to load than graphic images of text.

On the other hand, graphic text can be set in any typeface you like, as the end viewer just sees a pixel image of your typesetting. There's also no limit to the size you can use; you can make an 800pt character as large as your screen if that is what the design calls for. The color of graphic text can be matched more reliably to other graphic items, and it can also be filled with textures and gradients as well as plain flat shades.

Using any graphics package to create text images is pretty simple, although it can still be a little frustrating to get sizes exactly right. Fireworks MX, in particular, is very well suited to making Web text graphics with visual bells and whistles.

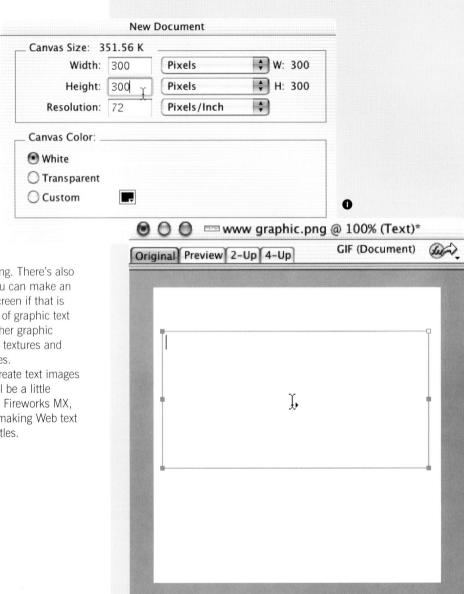

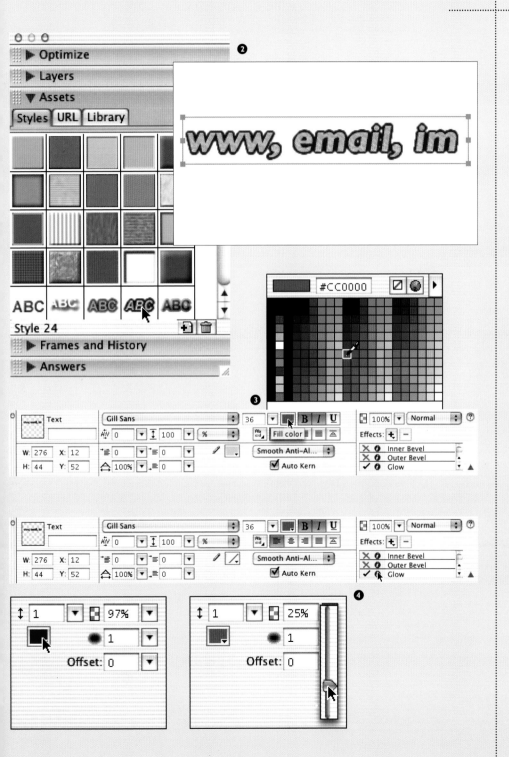

❶ Launch Fireworks and make a new document, at least 300 pixels wide and tall. Choose the *Text* tool, and then draw out a text box.

❷ Click inside and type "www, email, im" (im stands for "instant messaging"). Now select the text and open the *Assets* palette. Choose *Styles* from the *Window* menu if you can't see it. This holds a number of predefined styles. Here we have picked *Style 24*, then enlarged the type size and changed the font to Gill Sans—creating instant graphic text.

❸ To edit the color, go to the *Properties* palette and click the *Fill Color* swatch. To change the texture used in the fill, click the *Fill Options* button in the *Fill Color* pop-up panel. This shows a new panel, with pop-up menus listing different textures and antialiasing options. You should also change the *Text Outline Color* panel from pale blue to nothing.

❹ The outer color for this text is provided by the *Glow* effect, which came as part of the style we originally applied. In the *Properties* palette, over in the *Effects* section on the right, click the small "i" dot next to the *Glow* name. Now use the color swatch pop-up to pick the most appropriate color for your text. You will probably find it worth dropping the opacity down with the slider in the top-right of the *Glow* effect panel.

120

❺ When you are done, you are ready to export the image as a Web graphic (preferably as a GIF with transparency.) But first you should trim off the unnecessary parts of the graphic. For this, don't bother playing around with Fireworks' slicing feature. It's not perfect, and it would not stop you from accidentally trimming off part of the text glow, for example. Just select the text box and *Copy* it, then make a new document.

❻ The new document size will automatically be based on the size of the visible part of what you just copied, so click OK, then paste into the new document window.

❼ Now choose *Export Preview* from the *File* menu, and pick the settings you need. GIF is almost certainly the best format, and if you know the color of the destination page background, pick that from the *Matte* swatch pop-up. This makes sure that antialiasing is done using the appropriate background color, which helps to prevent obvious fringes from appearing around the edges of the text.

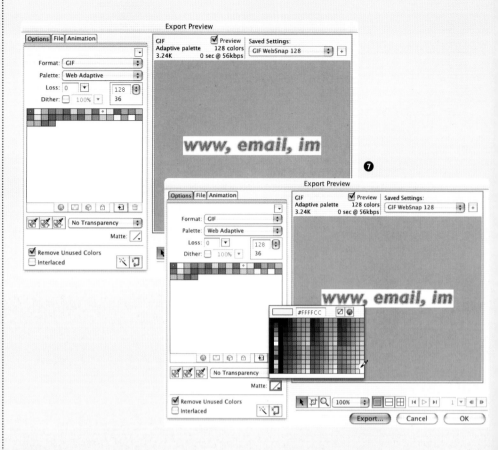

❺

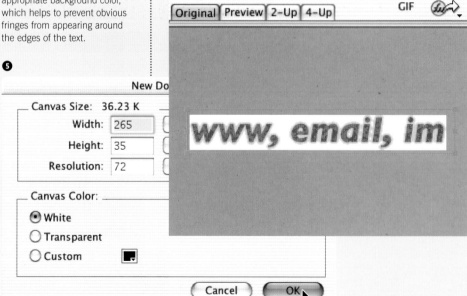

❻

❽

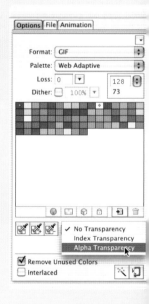

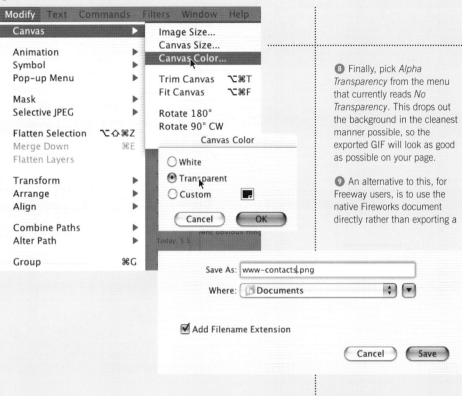

8 Finally, pick *Alpha Transparency* from the menu that currently reads *No Transparency*. This drops out the background in the cleanest manner possible, so the exported GIF will look as good as possible on your page.

9 An alternative to this, for Freeway users, is to use the native Fireworks document directly rather than exporting a

Web graphic as a separate file. First, go to *Canvas* in the *Modify* menu and choose *Canvas Color*. Select *Transparent* from the list of choices that comes up, then save the document to disk.

10 Fireworks uses the PNG format for its own files, so all variable transparency information is kept intact. Import the image into your layout, then place it wherever it needs to go. The graphic will blend transparently with whatever it covers, and the final output will default to either GIF or JPEG, fully compatible with all browsers.

11 If flat-color graphic text is what is wanted, just set it as normal in a graphics package, then crop it and export as a GIF. If you are working in Freeway, you could even click inside a graphic box and set the text from there. No external files are needed and any typesetting can be done in the page layout.

122

PROJECT 23
ROLLOVER GRAPHICS

Rollover graphics are simply items which, when pointed at (or clicked), show a different image. This common effect can be exploited in all sorts of ways, from the traditional "light up a button" effect in a navigation bar to playing creatively with image segments in an artful, fun way.

In a nutshell, a rollover is a set of instructions, built into the Web page, that swaps one image for another when something trips the trigger. The image to be shown appears in exactly the same place as the original. The "hot spot" trigger is usually placed in the page around the item being changed, but it is possible to have a rollover hot spot in one part of a page that changes something in another area.

The end product may be an old Web standard, but different programs handle rollover creation in very different ways. Photoshop uses ImageReady, its bundled specialist Web graphics tool, to create rollovers from image layers and "slice" shapes. Fireworks uses frames rather than layers, and Freeway uses actions applied to stacked graphic boxes. Dreamweaver and GoLive can also build rollovers themselves, as long as the relevant graphic images have already been made.

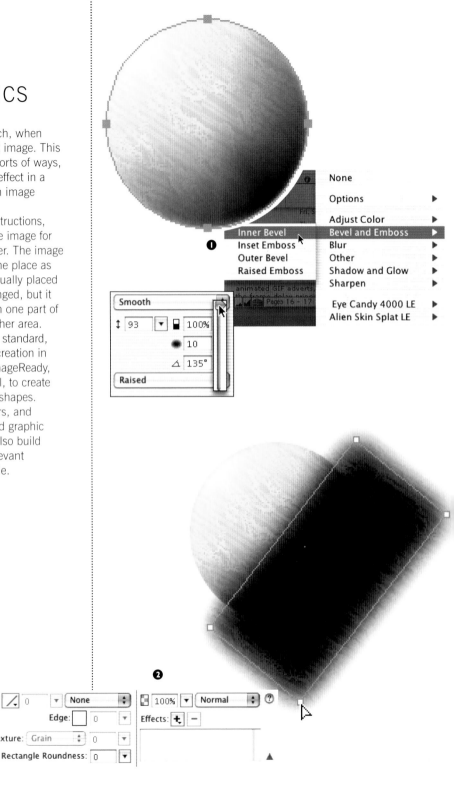

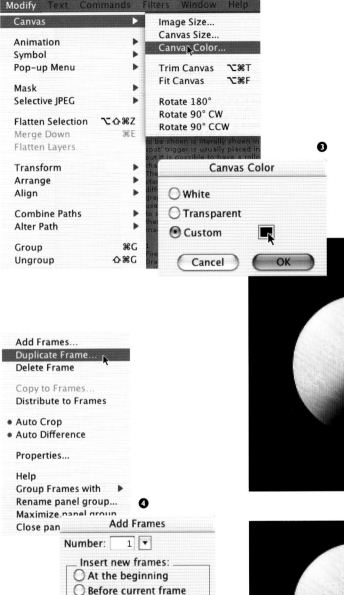

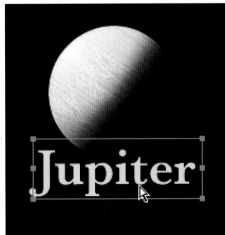

❶ Fireworks is great for creating graphics with special effects in next to no time. Draw a simple circle and, using the *Properties* palette, fill it with a sandy yellow fill color and an Onyx fill texture. Next add an *Inner Bevel* effect, again using the *Properties* palette, with the *Smooth* option selected, width set high, and contrast and softness at maximum.

❷ Draw a rectangle and fill it with black, then give it a 20% Onyx fill and set the edge to a 20-pixel feather. Make sure that the *Transparent* box is checked, then rotate and drag this so it provides a more extreme form of shading. The circle is ready to transform into a distant planet.

❸ Go to *Canvas* in the *Modify* menu and choose *Canvas Color*. Pick black from the custom pop-up swatch list and click OK.

❹ Now move over to the *Frames* palette. From the pop-up menu button in its top-right corner, choose *Duplicate Frame*. This creates a copy of the first frame, including all of that frame's elements.

❺ Use the *Text* tool to make a new text object, and type "Jupiter." Set this to be around 48 points and a pale sand color similar to the circle. Drag this under the large circle as if it were an oversized dot for the letter "i" in the text.

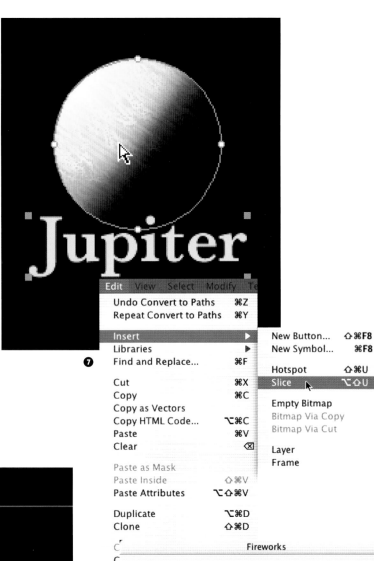

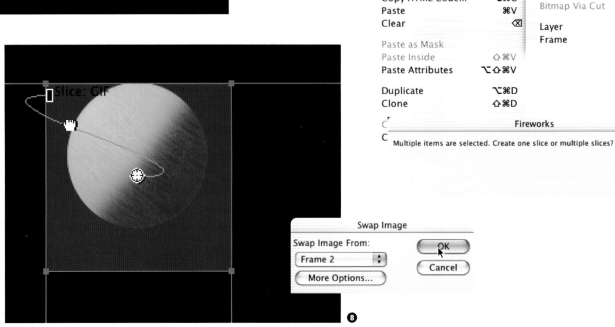

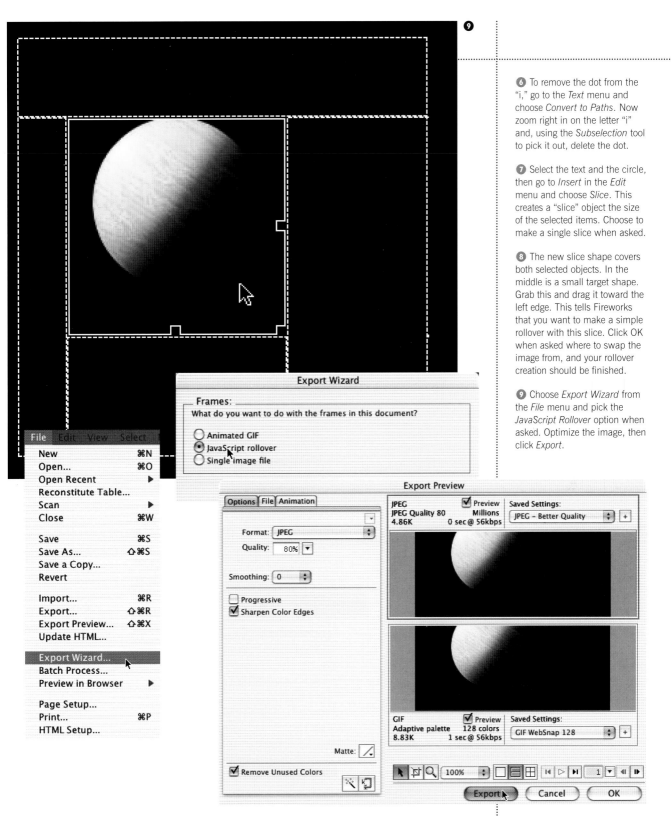

❻ To remove the dot from the "i," go to the *Text* menu and choose *Convert to Paths*. Now zoom right in on the letter "i" and, using the *Subselection* tool to pick it out, delete the dot.

❼ Select the text and the circle, then go to *Insert* in the *Edit* menu and choose *Slice*. This creates a "slice" object the size of the selected items. Choose to make a single slice when asked.

❽ The new slice shape covers both selected objects. In the middle is a small target shape. Grab this and drag it toward the left edge. This tells Fireworks that you want to make a simple rollover with this slice. Click OK when asked where to swap the image from, and your rollover creation should be finished.

❾ Choose *Export Wizard* from the *File* menu and pick the *JavaScript Rollover* option when asked. Optimize the image, then click *Export*.

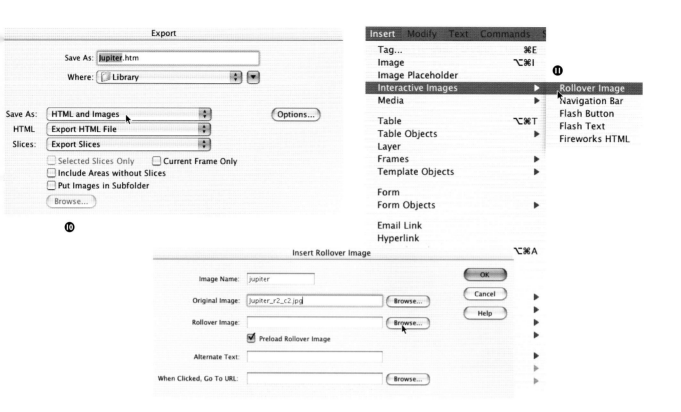

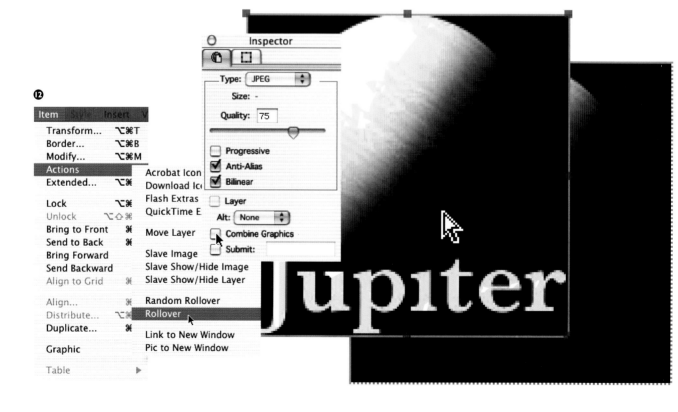

⑩ Now you're asked what to export. You can choose *HTML and Images*, to create a collection of files suitable for opening in Dreamweaver or GoLive, or you can just export the two images and use them in any Web design tool.

⑪ Dreamweaver Here Dreamweaver has been used to open the HTML file with the linked rollover graphic. Now it can be incorporated into a regular Web layout. To make a rollover from scratch using ready-made graphics, choose *Rollover Image* from *Interactive Images* in the *Insert* menu, then pick the two images to use.

⑫ Freeway Freeway's rollover creation uses graphic boxes stacked together. Make two graphic boxes and import the two images, then move them into position. To prevent them from being merged on final output (which can affect the behavior), uncheck the *Combine Graphics* box for them in the *Inspector* palette. Now go to *Actions* in the *Item* menu, and pick *Rollover*.

⑬ In the *Actions* palette, make sure to view the "columns" style interface, the second of the two small buttons. In the *Normal* column, uncheck the item to hide, and in the *Mouse* column, add a check for the item to show when the mouse is over the hot spot.

128

PROJECT 24

IMAGE SLICING

Image slicing is simply the process of taking a larger image and cutting it into smaller parts, which are then held in place by an HTML table so that the final appearance is of a single unsliced whole.

Image slicing is sometimes the only way to achieve a particular effect. This is the case when a section of a larger image is to be a rollover, changing in some way when a viewer points at or clicks on something. This is a popular technique with navigation bars—graphic elements that are sliced up to accommodate a number of different rollovers. Producing these constructs involves the same efforts as making basic rollovers (see Project 23), the only difference being the number of separate rollovers created.

In some cases, the reason for slicing up an image is because one part of a design strongly suits the JPEG file format and another part suits the GIF format. This is likely when trying to combine photographic and text graphics in one image, particularly when high compression levels are needed. If a visually complex and subtle image is combined with hard-edged graphic elements and type, a "one size fits all" approach to compression is rarely going to work well. The problem with doing this is the potential for color mismatch, so watch the divisions between formats very carefully.

Some Web designers absolutely love image slicing, using it whenever they get the chance. However, image slicing shouldn't be done for the sake of it. As the image is made up of multiple parts held together by a table structure, the final graphic takes multiple requests to the Web server to retrieve, and the more complex page structure can prove hard for Web browsers to handle. All the same, this is sometimes preferable to having a single large image that takes many seconds to retrieve. Just think of the user spending their time staring at a big empty space.

❹

❶ ImageReady This image has distinct sharp areas and areas that are soft with subtle changes in tone. Using ImageReady, it is clear that heavy JPEG compression would serious degrade the edges of the snowflake shapes.

❷ With the image set to GIF instead, the snowflake shapes are crisp, but the subtle shading in the photograph is rather unpleasantly simplified.

❸ Choose the *Slice* tool from the *Tool* palette. (Fireworks behaves in a similar way, although ImageReady uses a special *Slice Select* tool for moving slice objects around.)

❹ Draw out slice rectangles over anything that needs to be treated differently from the rest of the image. The door on the left won't survive the same heavy JPEG compression that the misty mountain needs, while the snowflakes need to be set to GIF format.

❺ Using the *Slice Select* tool (click and hold the *Slice* tool in the *Tool* palette to get this), select one of the slices, then use the *Optimize* palette to choose the settings. Information about how large the slice item will be is shown at the bottom of the image window, along with the current compression settings. If extreme settings are used, a clear difference will be seen between the areas when using the *Preview* display.

❺

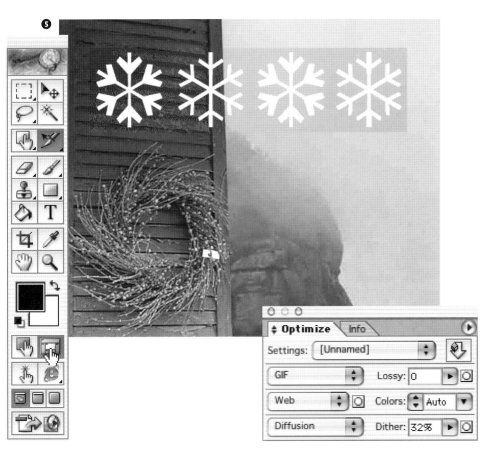

130

⑥ With the right balance of formats and compression settings, the result should look clean and still be fairly compact. This example uses heavy and medium JPEG compression, plus a limited-color GIF setting for the hard-edged graphics, and manages to be less than 30Kb in total.

⑦ **Freeway** The simple way of achieving the same effect in Freeway is to import the finished product as a single image, then draw out empty graphic blocks as slices. Uncheck the *Combine Graphics* checkbox in the *Inspector* palette so that the image will be chopped up with those shapes.

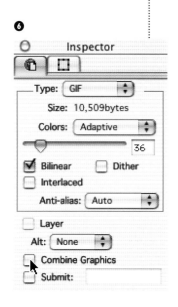

8

9

8 Finally, use the first pane in the *Inspector* palette to set the format and compression for each box. Turn on *Graphics Preview* in the *View* menu to see the effect of the compression and format settings. Try sending boxes in front and then behind those with different settings to see how this affects things.

9 Alternatively, you can import multiple elements from separate Photoshop files. Using cutout images on layers with empty, transparent backgrounds enables you to do the collaging from within the layout. Import the different image files into different graphic boxes, then arrange, scale, and crop them as necessary.

10 To set up slices, turn off *Combine Graphics* in the *Inspector* palette for selected boxes. Alternatively, draw new boxes over areas, and turn off *Combine Graphics* for those.

10

132 **PROJECT 15**
ANIMATED GIFS

Color in Web pages is generally a static thing, barring things like the JavaScript tricks we looked at earlier in the book. But the humble animated GIF file can put a sparkle into an otherwise dull page with relative ease, as well as catch the eye. The animated GIF file format is very straightforward; it is simply a series of GIF images stacked together, and shown by the Web browser one by one in sequence.

Creating an animation takes some planning, but one good general rule to remember is to keep it simple. This animated GIF trick uses a simple shape and the principles of silhouettes to create a basic but striking result. Finally, delaying the animation's start for a few seconds will mean that it suddenly appears when the viewer isn't expecting it. It wouldn't be good to try this with animated GIF adverts, where subtlety isn't generally too effective, but the frame-delay principle is well worth exploiting elsewhere.

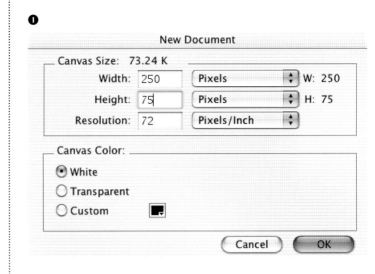

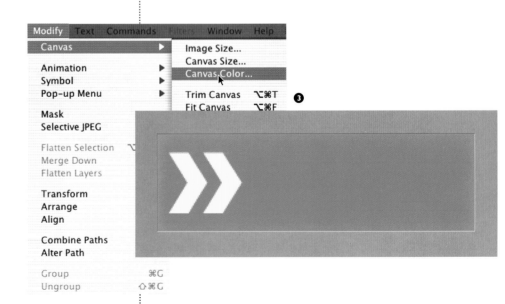

❶ Create a new document in Fireworks, making it the size you would want it to be in the page. This example is 250 pixels wide by 75 pixels tall.

❷ Use the *Text* tool to draw a box, then type a right-hand guillemet (the "»" character, which is the French closing quotation mark). With a UK or US Mac keyboard, this is typed with option-shift-\. Set this to a large size such as 96 points (the largest available via the slider), and use a strong, bold sans-serif font. Here we have used Gill Sans Bold. Place it on the left of the canvas.

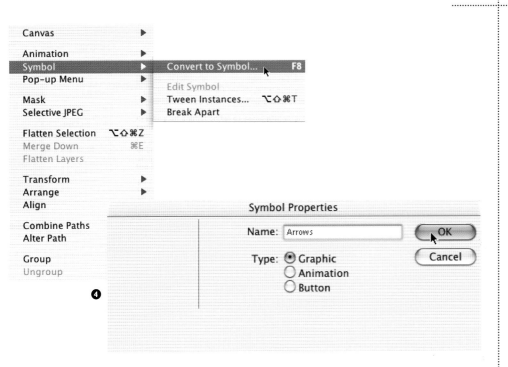

❸ Now use the *Fill Color* picker in the *Properties* palette to set the text to the same color as the final page. As this is likely to make the object virtually or totally vanish, you will also need to set the canvas color to something different; go to *Canvas* in the *Modify* menu and pick *Canvas Color*. Choose a mid-strength color rather than black, as we will be working with drop shadows shortly.

❹ Select the text box, then go to *Symbol* in the *Modify* menu and choose *Convert to Symbol*. Call it *Arrows*, and click OK.

❺ Choose *Clone* from the *Edit* menu to create a copy of the new symbol on top of the original. Then grab it with the mouse, hold down the shift key, and drag it to the other side of the canvas.

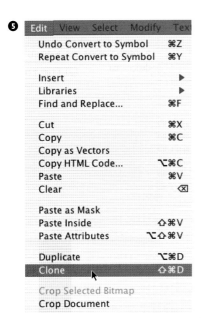

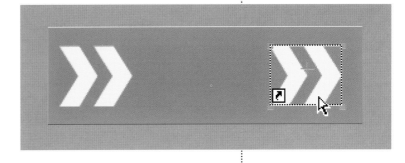

134

6 With the second symbol selected, click the '+' button in the *Effects* section of the *Properties* palette. Go to *Shadow and Glow*, and choose *Drop Shadow*.

7 In the *Drop Shadow* settings panel that appears, set the opacity slider to 80%, the softness to 15, and the angle to 270 degrees.

8 You will probably need to shift the objects up in the canvas to avoid them being clipped, so shift-click to select them both, then drag them up so they fit in the space. Now give the first symbol a drop shadow, but set its distance and softness to zero so it is hidden.

9 These elements are the beginning and end points of the simple animation—we can make Fireworks produce all the in-between steps. Go to *Modify>Symbol>Tween Instances*. In the *Tween Instances* dialog, choose eight tween steps (to end up with a total of ten), and click the *Distribute to Frames* checkbox.

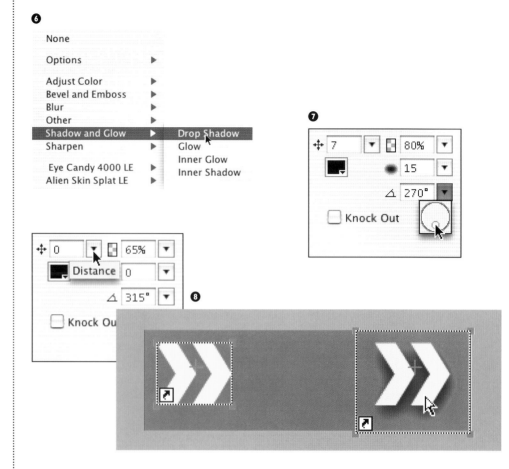

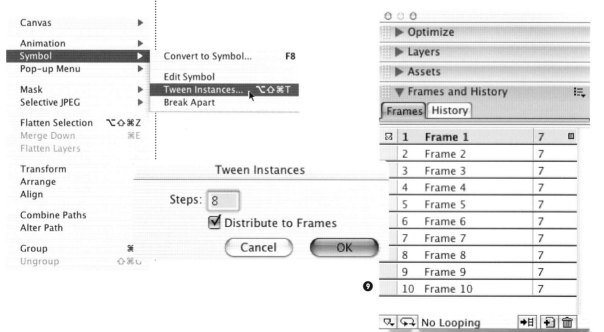

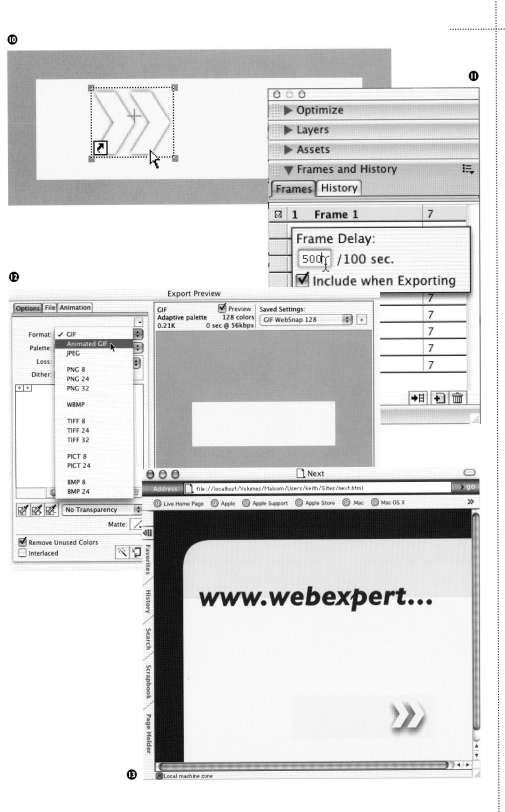

❿ Use the *Canvas Color* setting to change the background to the same as your page. Now you may notice a slight fringe of shadow around the shape on the first frame. Select the object, then set its opacity to zero with the slider in the *Properties* palette. Click the second frame in the *Frames* palette, and set that object's opacity to 25%. Make the third 50% opaque and the fourth 75% opaque, and the effect is much better.

⓫ Now you can click the play button at the bottom-left of the document window. The animation immediately kicks off, and loops over and over. Click the button next to *Forever* in the bottom of this palette and pick *No Looping*. To make the first frame pause for five seconds, click the "7" in the first frame, in the *Frames* palette. Change the delay to 500.

⓬ Finally, pick *Export Preview* from the File menu, then select Animated GIF from the *Format* pop-up menu. Test the playback with the animation controller buttons, then click *Export*.

⓭ Now place your new animated GIF in a Web page, just like you would any other Web graphic. When you view the page in a Web browser, it will wait for five seconds and then play, fading in and across the background. When it gets to the last frame, it will stop.

136 **PROJECT 26**

ANIMATED BACKGROUND GRAPHICS

Animated GIFs are almost always used for regular graphic objects in a page layout, but they can also be used as a page background image.

Background images normally tile across and down to fill the Web browser window, repeating the picture as much as necessary. It is possible to use JavaScript commands to control this, making the image tile only across or down, or not at all. In most cases, this isn't a good trick to use, as the rest of the page is then left unadorned. Sometimes, however, with the right graphic, this can be worth exploiting.

Using an animated graphic as a page background is almost always going to be a bad idea. After all, if one bouncing ball graphic is bad enough, how unpleasant would a whole page of them be? But with a more creative approach to animation, particularly with a definite end result in mind, you should be able to produce something intriguing, rather than just irritating.

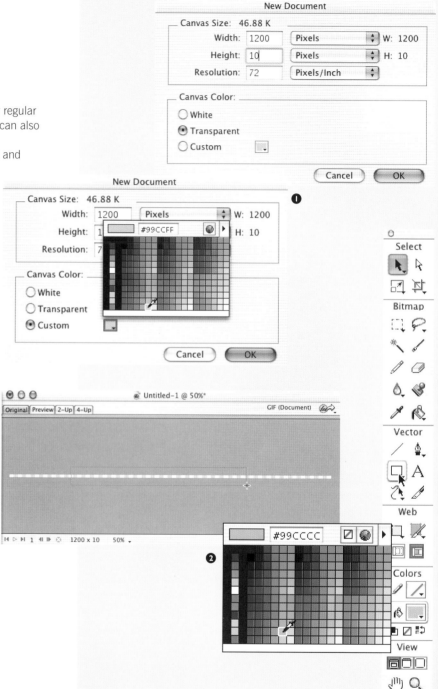

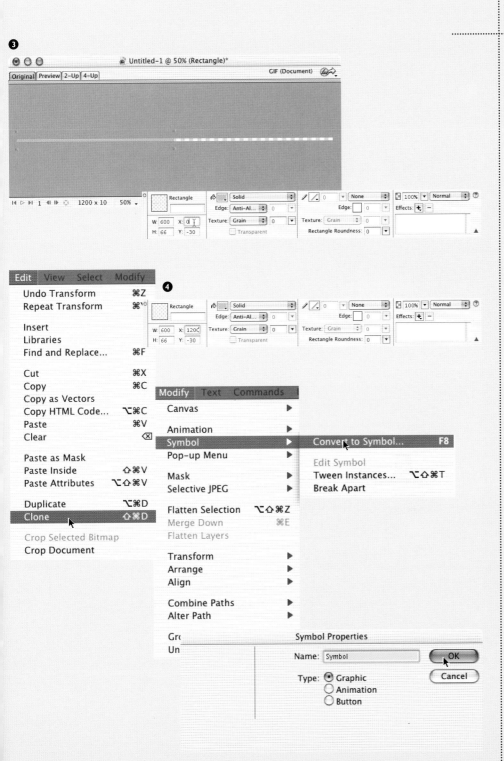

① Start off by making an animation in Fireworks. Create a document that is 1200 pixels wide by just 10 pixels tall, and has a transparent canvas. You may need to adjust the zoom of the window in order to see the full width comfortably.

② Now draw out a rectangle about half the width of the whole canvas, and give it a fill color using the *Properties* palette. This animation needs to be fairly subtle or the final effect will be overwhelming, so pick a pale gray-blue, #99CCCC, from the lower-left set of colors in the *Color* panel.

③ Using the *Properties* palette's measurements section on the left, set the X (horizontal) position of the rectangle to 0. We are about to animate this moving across the canvas, but to make this loop smoothly, we also need a second block.

④ Choose *Clone* from the *Edit* menu, then use the *Properties* palette to move this rectangle the full 1200 pixel width of the canvas. Now choose *Select All* from the *Edit* menu, then, go to *Modify>Symbol>Convert to Symbol*. Choose *Graphic* and then click *OK*.

138

⑤ The two rectangles (you can see only one, but both were selected) have been turned into a single "symbol." With this selected, choose *Clone* again, then use the *Properties* palette to set the X position of the new symbol to 1200.

⑥ Now choose *Select All*, then choose *Modify> Symbol> Tween Instances* once again. Create 49 steps, and click the *Release to Frames* checkbox.

⑦ In the *Frames* palette, click the last frame—frame 51—and click the trash can button to delete it. This leaves you with a smoothly looping animation; click the *Play* button in the bottom-left of the document window to see how it looks.

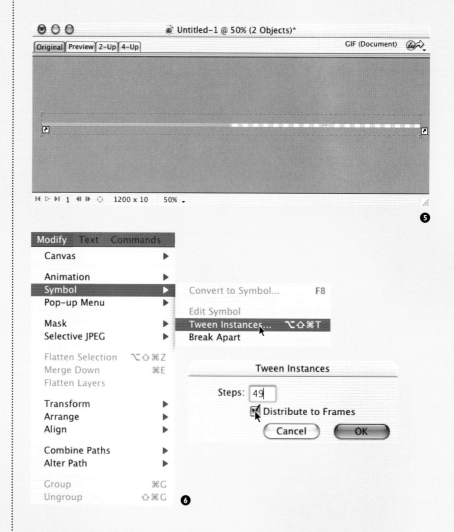

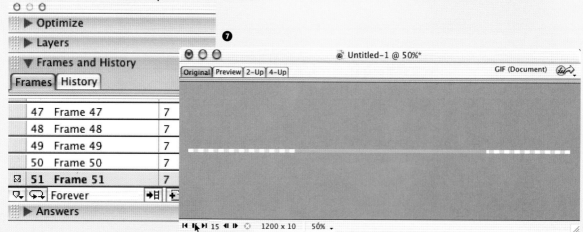

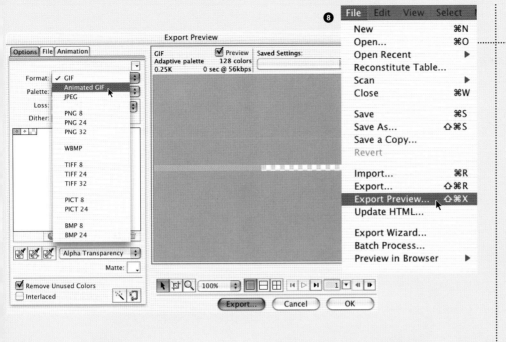

8 Finally, choose *Export Preview* from the *File* menu and pick Animated GIF from the *Format* menu. Click *Export*, and your work will be saved to disk as a GIF animation.

9 Now make a couple more of these; start again from step 1 with a new 1200x10 pixel document, but this time make four 100-pixel wide, evenly spaced rectangles, filled with a color resembling #66CCCC, placed at 300, 600, 900, and 1200 pixels.

10 Select all the blocks and convert them to a graphic symbol, as in step 4. Then *Clone* this symbol and move the blocks 300 pixels to the left. Finally, select both symbols, and follow steps 6 to 8.

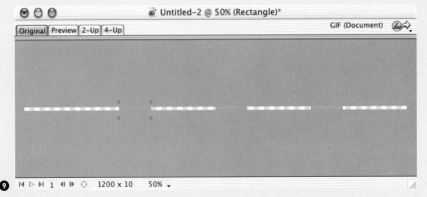

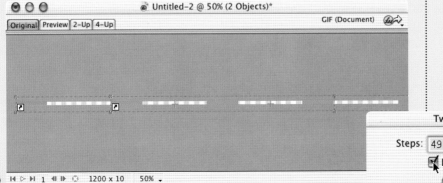

140

⑪ Now, in another new 1200x10 pixel document, make a 200-pixel wide block placed at 0. Fill it with white, then clone and move it to 600. Then *Select All* and *Convert to Symbol*, *Clone* again, and move the new symbol to 600. Finally, follow steps 6 to 8 again.

⑫ Still with us? You can close the documents you have just made. We need one final new document, the same 1200 pixels wide by 10 pixels tall, but this time with a canvas color of #99CCFF, a light grayish blue.

⑬ Import the three animated GIFs you just made, letting new frames be added automatically when asked. Now open the *Library* palette, from the *Window* menu if necessary, and you will see the three animations listed.

⑭ Select each one in turn in the main window, and use the *Properties* palette to set the start and end points to 50% opacity. When you try the *Play* button, you should get an idea of how this will look. Now choose *Export Preview* from the *File* menu, select the Animated GIF format, and click *Export*.

⑮ Use any website design program—Dreamweaver, GoLive, or Freeway—to use this new GIF as a page background image. When it is viewed in a Web browser, the vertical stripes will dance back and forth across the page in a surprisingly mesmerizing manner. You should also see why picking subdued, almost dull colors is a good start, as the movement turns the subtle tones into something almost loud again.

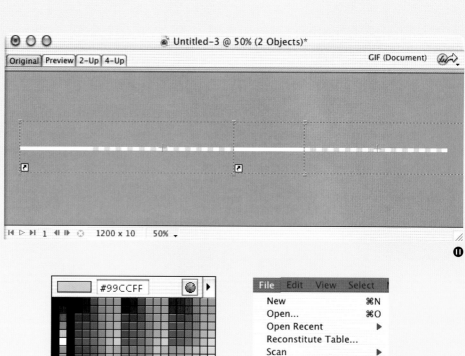

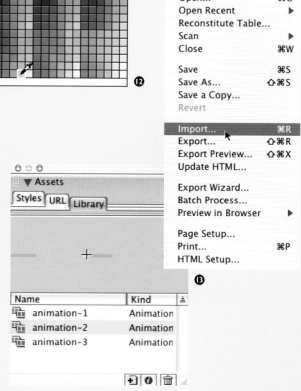

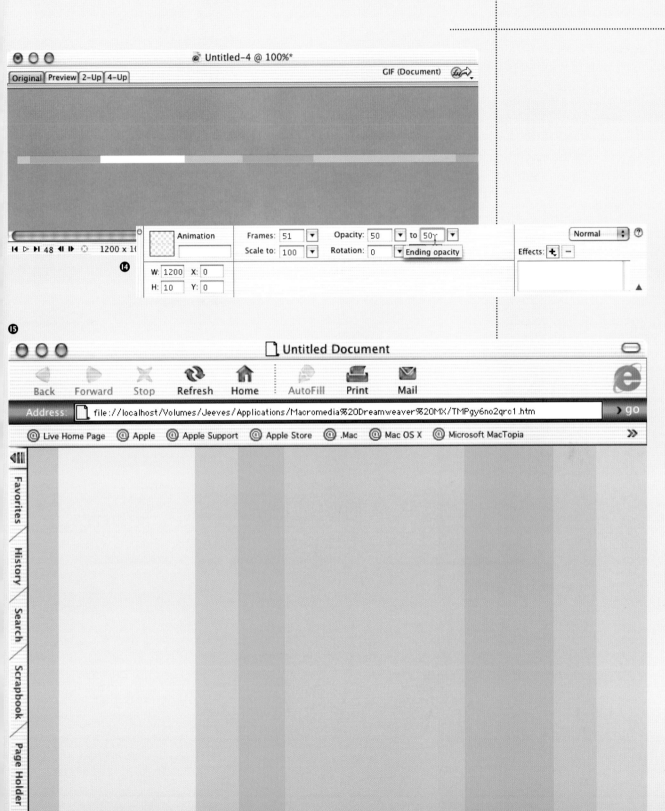

142 **PROJECT 27**

DITHERED GRAPHICS AND BACKGROUND ANIMATIONS

The previous project showed how to create an animated GIF with a difference, designed specifically for use as a page background image. The next logical step is to create graphics that feel as much a part of this dynamic page as the background does, by creating foreground images which visually blend in and out of the background as the animation cycles through.

Two tricks are used in this project. First of all, matching the color used in part of the animation makes an item sink into the background as that shade passes by. And second, by using GIF transparency and a pixel-sized grille of transparent and opaque colors, any background colors will show through the object.

The result can be something that feels like a complex Flash-based extravaganza, but which is built using nothing but basic Web graphics and a little lateral thinking. It can take practice getting the color balance right in this one, but the effect makes all that effort worthwhile.

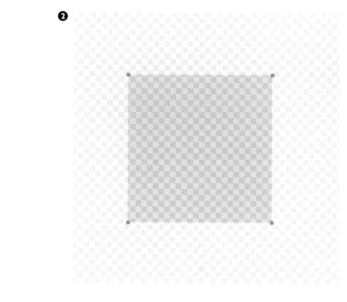

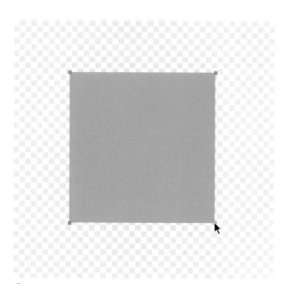

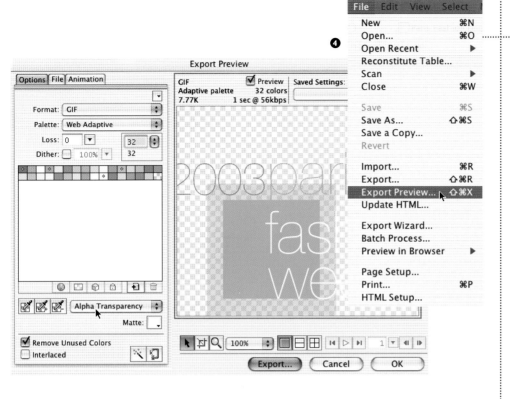

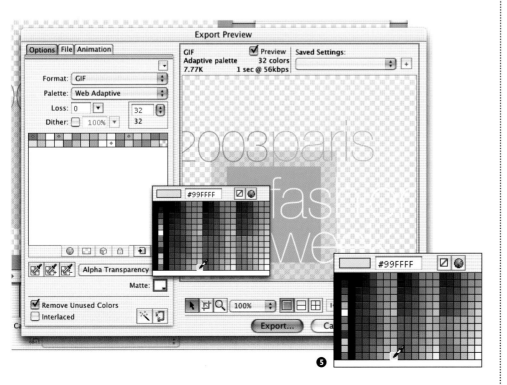

1 Make a new Fireworks document, 400x400 pixels in size and with a transparent background. Draw a rectangle 200 pixels square, and fill it with the darkest color used in the previous project.

2 Use the *Properties* palette to set the texture to "Grid 3," and the texture's transparency to 100%. The resulting fill should be a pixel-level grid of color and transparency. Other grids will probably achieve similar results, but this one manages to be both extremely fine and an even 50-50 split in terms of transparent and opaque pixels.

3 Now add whatever graphic and type extras you want, but keep things relatively simple. Fancy effects such as shadows and embossing are not likely to work too well, but cool, carefully placed graphic shapes probably will. You can experiment later, but for now remember to stick to a general color scheme that matches the hues you used in the animation.

4 Once the graphic layout is finished, it is time to export the work for use in the Web page. Choose *Export Preview* from the *File* menu, and make sure to choose the GIF format and enable transparency.

5 Any graphic edge, particularly on curved shapes such as type, will have a measure of antialiasing. The matte color used in the antialias blending should be set to the predominant color of the animated GIF background. Use the *Matte* pop-up color panel to choose this.

6

7

❽

shion
eek

зoзparis

fashion
week

photo

fashion
week

❻ Now place it in the Web page, in a page that has an animated GIF set as the backgound image. This background image was built using the principles of the previous project, but with slightly different colors and shapes. If you use Freeway, be sure not to scale or rotate this foreground image; if it is resampled at any stage, the pixel grid transparency effect will not work properly.

❼ The result, when viewed in a Web browser, should be extremely effective. What is more, it will work in just about any graphics-capable Web browser around, without requiring either a single rich media plug-in or large amounts of memory.

❽ The next step would be to add rollovers that use the same color as parts of the animation, possibly with transparent grid areas as well if the design called for it. The possibilities are endless, from dynamic pop-art extravaganzas to slow, subtle blended changes.

146 PROJECT 28
TRANSPARENT PNG EFFECTS

Combining transparent graphics and scripts that make things draggable can lead to some rather exciting possibilities. This project makes use of a transparent PNG file that mimics a magnifying glass. It cannot actually distort what shows through the "glass" of course, but the effect is still enough to make the casual observer unsure. We also use dragging to let the user peer around the page, and a snap-to JavaScript that helps them locate the hidden information and changes the page color as well.

Make sure that the overall effect is going to be worth the fuss of using this format. PNG files are often slightly larger than their GIF or JPEG equivalent, and when a transparency mask is involved, this difference becomes even bigger. If this is what you want, then carry on; there's just no good alternative. Just make sure not to use very large images if you don't expect most of your audience to have high-speed Internet connections.

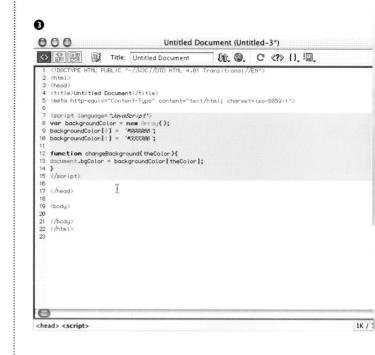

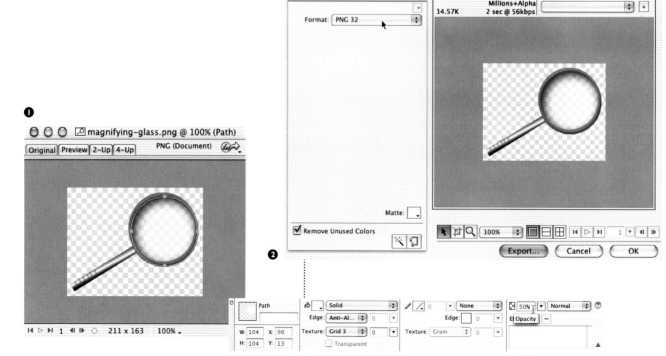

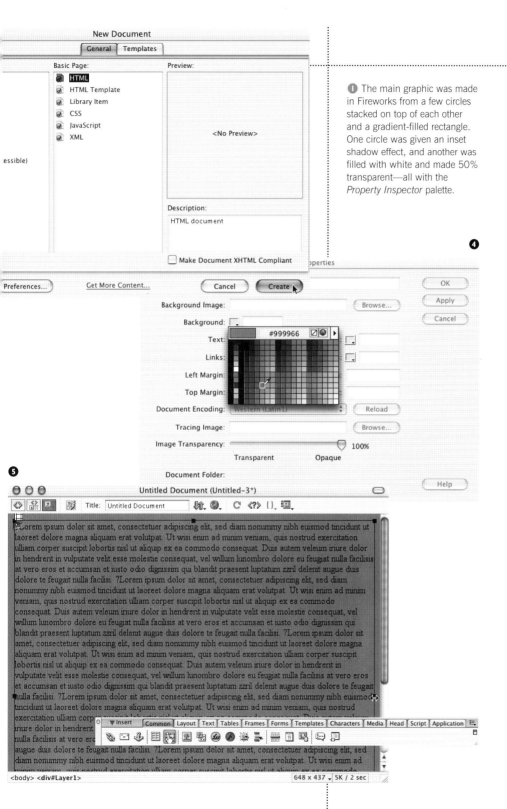

❶ The main graphic was made in Fireworks from a few circles stacked on top of each other and a gradient-filled rectangle. One circle was given an inset shadow effect, and another was filled with white and made 50% transparent—all with the *Property Inspector* palette.

❷ With the construction on a transparent canvas, the next step is to export as the right kind of PNG file. Choose *Export Preview* from the *File* menu and choose PNG 32 from the *Format* pop-up menu. Click *Export*, and it is time to move across to Dreamweaver.

❸ Make a new Dreamweaver document. Remember the JavaScript code we used in project 4? We are going to make use of that again, so click the *Show Code View* button at the top-left of the Dreamweaver document window, then click just before the </head> line and type a return to get a new line. Type the script shown below so it appears before the </head> line.

```
<script
 language="JavaScript">
var backgroundColor =
 new Array();
backgroundColor[0] =
 '#999966';
backgroundColor[1] =
 '#333300';

function
 changeBackground(theColor)
 {
document.bgColor =
 backgroundColor[theColor];
 }
</script>
```

❹ Now click the *Show Design View* button. Go to the *Modify* menu and choose *Page Properties*, then set the background color to #999966.

❺ Click the *Draw Layer* button in the *Insert* toolbar and drag out a layer shape. Click in it, then type enough random text, to fill most of the window. Alternatively, you can download, *Copy* and *Paste* the Lorem Ipsum "dummy text" text file from www.webexpert.com.

148

⑥ Open the *CSS Styles* palette (choose it in the *Window* menu if necessary), and click the *New Style* button. Pick *Make Custom Style*, then click *OK*. In the *Style Definition* window, pick *Type*, then set the font to the Verdana set and the size to 10 pixels. Set the color to #CCCC66. Finally, select all the text and click the new style in the *CSS Styles* palette.

⑦ Draw out another layer and click inside it, then choose *Image* from the *Insert* menu. Navigate to where you saved the PNG graphic and choose that. Don't worry about the slightly crude display in Dreamweaver—this program isn't very good at showing certain kinds of graphics.

⑧ Now pick a few words perhaps a quarter of the way down the screen and change them to read "Telephone" and your telephone number, or something of the sort. Drag the magnifying glass layer across to this text, placing the lens area over the number.

⑨ The final appearance is determined by the Web browser, so press F12 on your keyboard to take a quick preview peek. As you can see, the PNG graphic looks much better here. Check the position of the magnifying glass and the "telephone" text, as the position of one or both may need to be adjusted.

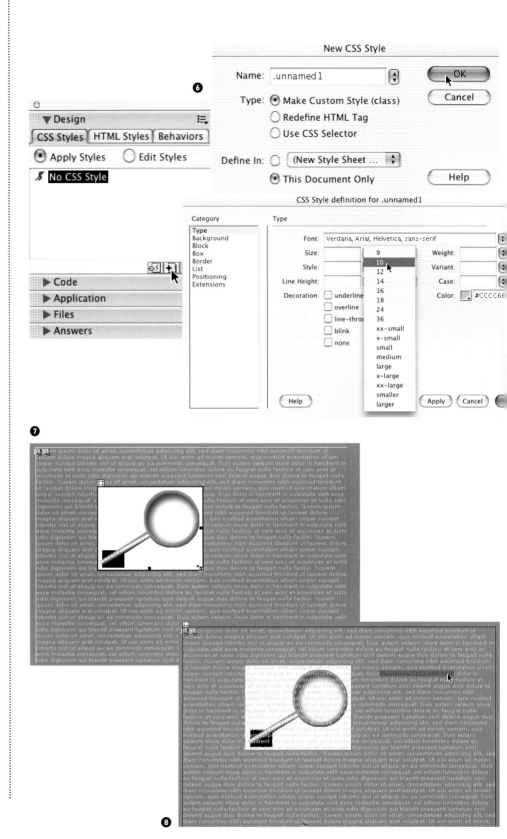

9

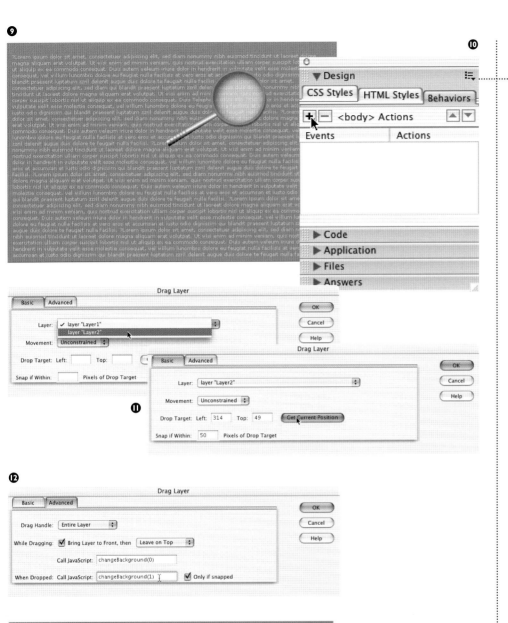

10

10 Now make the graphic layer draggable. Open the *Behaviors* palette and, making sure you don't have any layer selected, click the "plus" button and pick *Drag Layer* from the list.

11 Pick the second layer (the one with the PNG graphic), then click the *Get Current Position* button. This assigns a position for the "snap-to" location in the browser, so if a user drags the item nearby and lets go, it jumps to that spot.

12 Finally, the part which uses the JavaScript from step 1: click the *Advanced* tab, then click in the first JavaScript text box and type "changeBackground(0)" (without the quotation marks). This script is called when someone drags the graphic, but the color it produces is the same as the original page color. Next, type "changeBackground(1)" into the second JavaScript text box. This is called when the layer is dropped. Make sure the *Only if snapped* checkbox is checked, and you're done.

13 Now move the magnifying glass to a different part of the page, and preview it in a browser. When someone drags the magnifying glass graphic around the page, they see the text through the lens (and all around as well). When they let it go in roughly the right place, it snaps into position and the page background color changes to highlight your text.

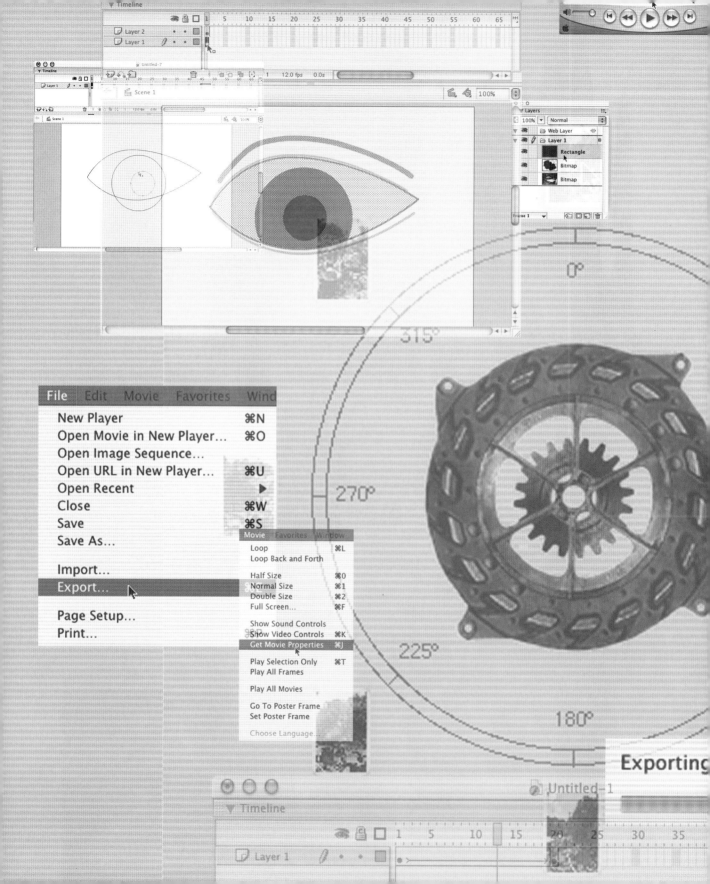

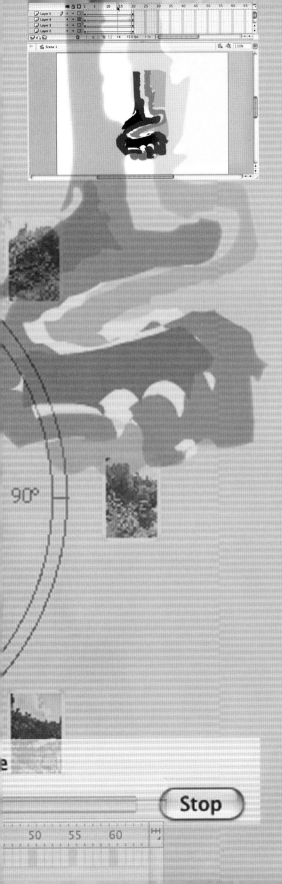

Plug-in Color

Plug-in media is anything that requires a Web browser "plug-in": a small program that enables you to see or hear video, audio, animation, or any other "rich media" in a Web page.

These projects begin by showing you ways to work with color in Flash movies, from converting images to Flash shapes right through to forcing the movie's background to fit in with the rest of your page.

We will also cover QuickTime, showing you how to blend movies into Web pages, or produce optimized, color-balanced VR panoramas. None of these projects are difficult, and each could add magic to your website.

152 PROJECT 29
COLOR IN FLASH

Macromedia Flash is a stunning program, capable of turning out incredibly rich, interactive animated media for Web use. In the hands of a skilled programmer, it can perform all sorts of scripted tricks, and yet the basics of controlling color in a Flash movie can be easily overlooked.

Treat Flash as a graphics tool when creating visual elements, but be ready to deal with its idiosyncratic way of handling objects. Shapes will cut holes into other shapes at the drop of a hat, and outlines can easily be separated from their inner shapes. It can be a fun way to make graphics, but it is certainly not like any other program. Flash can be hard to control at time, but a judicious use of layers helps, as does converting editable shapes into "symbol" objects and using the right tools for each task. There are a fair number of these tools to choose from: an oval graphic tool; a rectangle tool; a pen tool for drawing custom shapes; a simple line tool and pencil and brush tools for freeform painting and drawing. The good news is that adding color to your Flash graphics is not hard, even if the fill and stroke of shapes become detached on occasion.

If this all gets too hard to handle, you may find it much easier to produce your Flash graphics in a tool such as Macromedia FreeHand and then export them for animating Flash. Alternatively, Adobe's Flash rival, LiveMotion, offers more traditional drawing tools, but still outputs Flash-format movies. It might not offer the same level of programming abilities, but that is less of a concern if graphics production is your main objective.

In this first Flash project we will just create a very simple graphic, ready to be animated later.

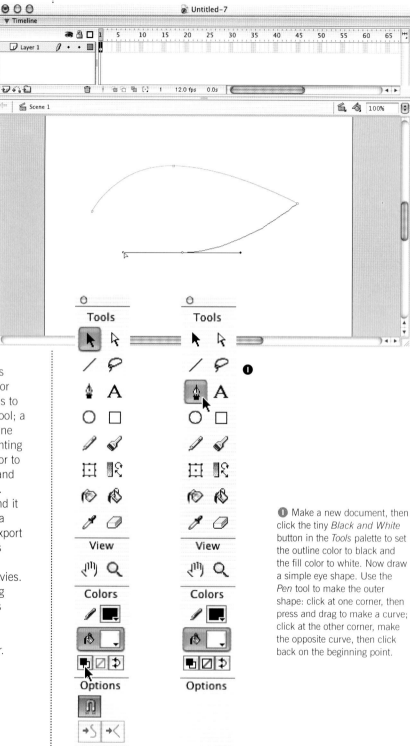

❶ Make a new document, then click the tiny *Black and White* button in the *Tools* palette to set the outline color to black and the fill color to white. Now draw a simple eye shape. Use the *Pen* tool to make the outer shape: click at one corner, then press and drag to make a curve; click at the other corner, make the opposite curve, then click back on the beginning point.

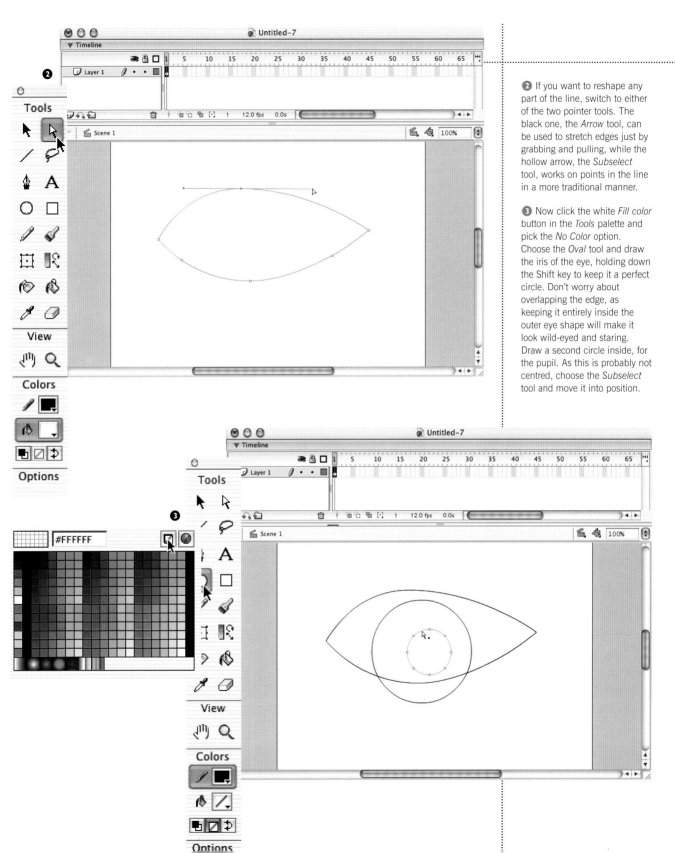

❷ If you want to reshape any part of the line, switch to either of the two pointer tools. The black one, the *Arrow* tool, can be used to stretch edges just by grabbing and pulling, while the hollow arrow, the *Subselect* tool, works on points in the line in a more traditional manner.

❸ Now click the white *Fill color* button in the *Tools* palette and pick the *No Color* option. Choose the *Oval* tool and draw the iris of the eye, holding down the Shift key to keep it a perfect circle. Don't worry about overlapping the edge, as keeping it entirely inside the outer eye shape will make it look wild-eyed and staring. Draw a second circle inside, for the pupil. As this is probably not centred, choose the *Subselect* tool and move it into position.

154

④ Choose the solid black *Arrow* tool and click on the portion of the circle that sticks out past the eye edges. This selects just that segment of line, so you can simply press the Delete key on the keyboard to get rid of it.

⑤ Now we can start coloring in the parts of the eye. Pick a strong blue from the *Fill Color* picker (here we use #336699), choose the *Fill* tool from the *Tools* palette, then click inside the outer circle. Fill the pupil in with black in the same manner.

⑥ Next, fill the outline around the blue iris with the same blue. Using the *Arrow* tool, click on the black outline to select it, then pick the appropriate color from the *Stroke* colors in the *Tools* palette.

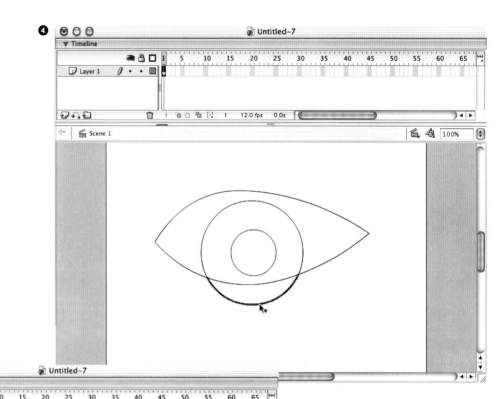

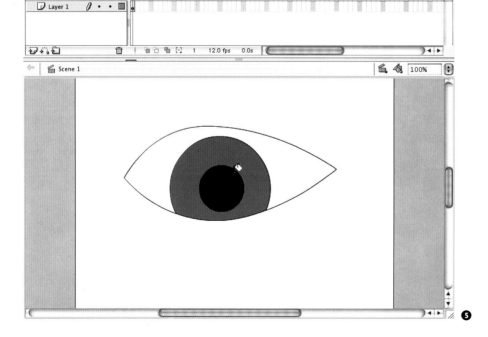

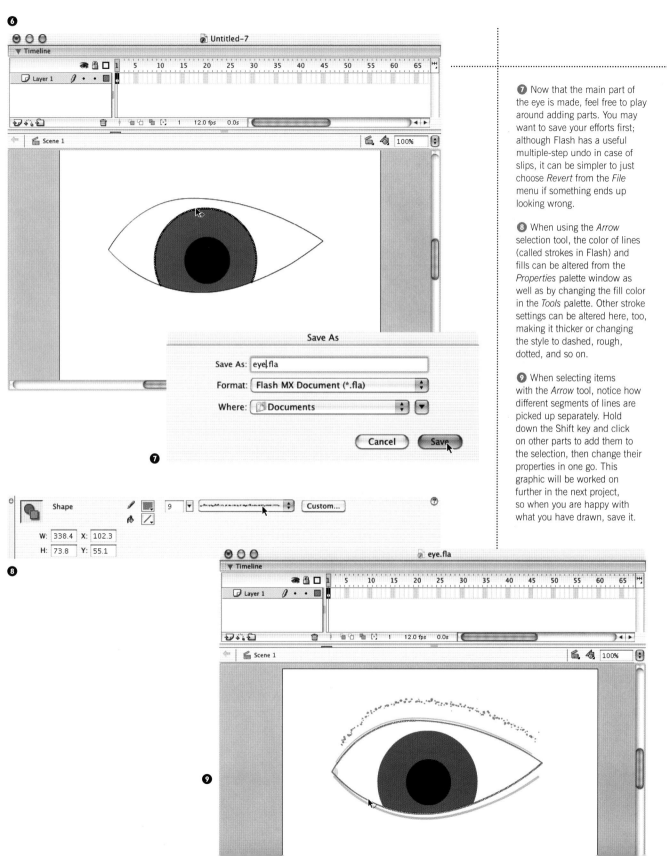

7 Now that the main part of the eye is made, feel free to play around adding parts. You may want to save your efforts first; although Flash has a useful multiple-step undo in case of slips, it can be simpler to just choose *Revert* from the *File* menu if something ends up looking wrong.

8 When using the *Arrow* selection tool, the color of lines (called strokes in Flash) and fills can be altered from the *Properties* palette window as well as by changing the fill color in the *Tools* palette. Other stroke settings can be altered here, too, making it thicker or changing the style to dashed, rough, dotted, and so on.

9 When selecting items with the *Arrow* tool, notice how different segments of lines are picked up separately. Hold down the Shift key and click on other parts to add them to the selection, then change their properties in one go. This graphic will be worked on further in the next project, so when you are happy with what you have drawn, save it.

156 PROJECT 30

ANIMATING SHAPES AND COLORS

Flash is a highly capable animation program, but moving items around the screen is just one of its abilities. Creating an animated morph of one item changing into another is a classic Flash party trick, and can be used to blend shape, color, and position with relative ease. How far this feature can go depends entirely on your imagination and drawing skills; it is extraordinarily flexible, and makes short work of animation tricks that used to take skilled artists days or even weeks to pull off.

Creating a tween animation requires following a set of steps in specific order. It isn't hard, but it must be done in a certain way to work predictably. Once you have a few such animations under your belt, the frustration fades away and it all seems obvious.

Remember that this tweening ability will work only with regular drawn Flash shapes, so any bitmaps have to be converted into native drawn Flash graphics using a bitmap tracing feature: see the next project for details.

❶ Open the Eye document from project 30. To keep your work safe, go to the *File* menu and choose *Save As*, then name this *Eye Morph*. Now we can work on this, knowing that there's a safe copy of the first project's result.

❷ Click the black pupil part of the eye with the *Arrow* tool to select it, then choose *Cut* from the *Edit* menu. This leaves the stroke behind, but we will deal with that in a moment.

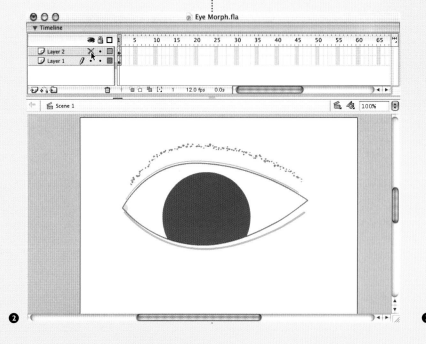

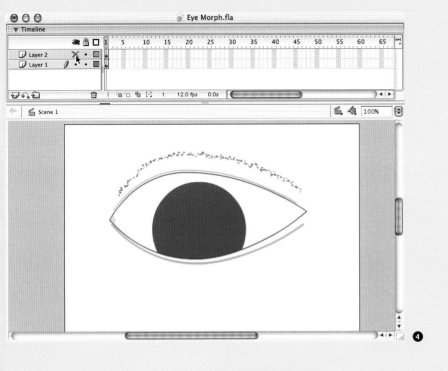

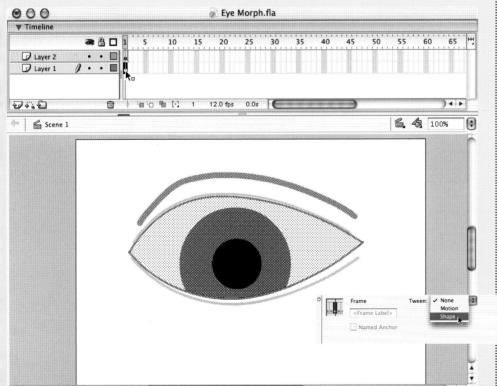

❸ Go to the *Insert* menu and choose *Layer*, then choose *Paste In Place* from the *Edit* menu. This pastes the pupil shape you just cut from the drawing back into the same relative location, but on the new layer. Now, in the *Layers* part of the Timeline at the top of the main window, click the dot in the "visible" column (the one with the eye) to hide layer 2.

❹ Click on Layer 1 to make it active (the pencil icon should appear in that layer bar). Click in an empty part of the canvas to deselect everything, then click the stroke left behind when we removed the pupil. Delete this, then fill the empty space with the same blue as the iris. Finally, show the pupil layer again. Now we will begin the morph part of the project.

❺ Click on the first keyframe in the layer 1 timeline at the top of the main window, then go to the *Tween* pop-up menu in the *Properties* palette. Now pick *Shape* from the options listed. You can alter how to ease-in and ease-out of the animation with the *Ease* control. To start slowly and speed up as it goes, pick a negative number. To keep things playing evenly, leave it set to zero.

If you want to blend graphics that are entirely or mainly straight lines and corners, pick *Angular* from the *Blend* pop-up menu. Otherwise—as in this case—leave it at *Distributive*.

158

⑥ Now click in the frame where the animation should end. For a 20 frame morph, simply click 20 frames along. Choose *Insert>**Keyframe*** from the menu, and all of the frames between the start and end keyframes will be filled in. Now change the color of the iris from blue to brown by selecting it with the *Arrow* tool and then selecting an appropriate color from the color picker in the *Tools* palette.

⑦ When you are happy with the color, try dragging the playhead marker in the timeline to an intermediate frame in the tween. You should see the half-way state between the start and end iris colors. Choose *Control>Play* or just press the return key to start the animation. If you are not happy with either of the initial graphics, go to the beginning or end frame of the tween and make your changes.

⑥

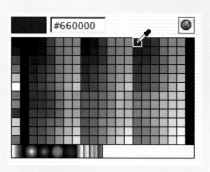

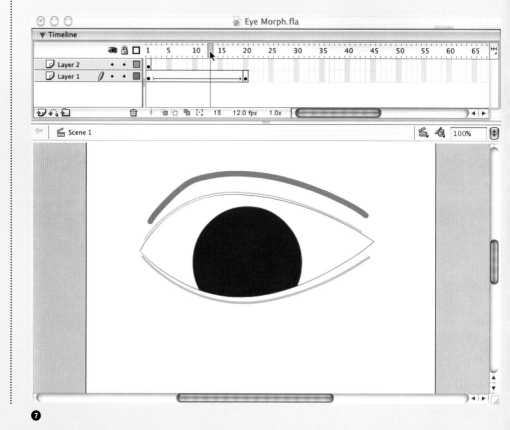

⑦

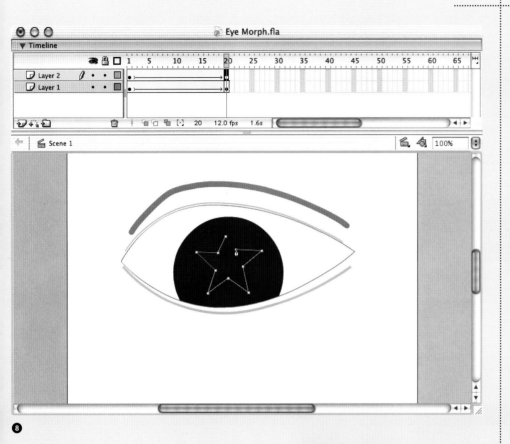

❽ The final morph is to change the shape of the pupil from the ordinary circle to a star. Click the single keyframe shown in the second layer, then pick *Shape* from the *Properties* palette's *Tween* options, click frame 20 in that layer and insert a new keyframe, just as you did in step six. Now select and delete the pupil shape from frame 20 and use the *Pen* tool to draw a basic star shape. Use the *Arrow* tool to select and delete the stroke. Next select the *Paint Bucket* tool, then pick the black-to-white radial fill in the *Properties* palette, and click in the new star shape. Now the animation will change the color of the eye and also morph the pupil from a regular black circle to a radial-filled star.

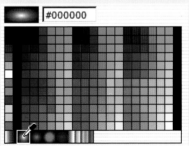

160

PROJECT 31
COMPLEX COLOR MORPHS

Simple morphs, such as changing a blue circle into a red square can be done in seconds. More complex shape changes demand more care and attention and can give unexpected results should the wrong parts deform across the tween. To control this, you will have to use a feature called "shape hints:" small markers that show the program which parts of the start and end point shapes correspond. In theory, Flash will look at the shape hints, then use the appropriate parts of the graphic when changing one item into another.

In practice, even shape hints don't always cure things. If not, try changing their positions or—in particularly stubborn cases—consider redrawing sections in different layers, then building separate tweens for each and every part.

❶ Here the shape tween is meant to change this set of rectangles into the stylized fist graphic. With no shape hints applied the result looks bizarre, as you can see from the mid-tween frame on the right.

❶

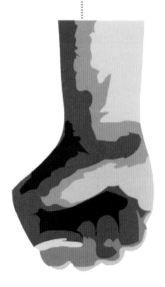

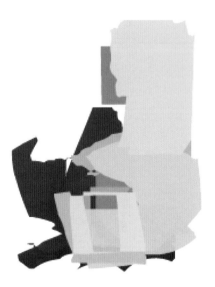

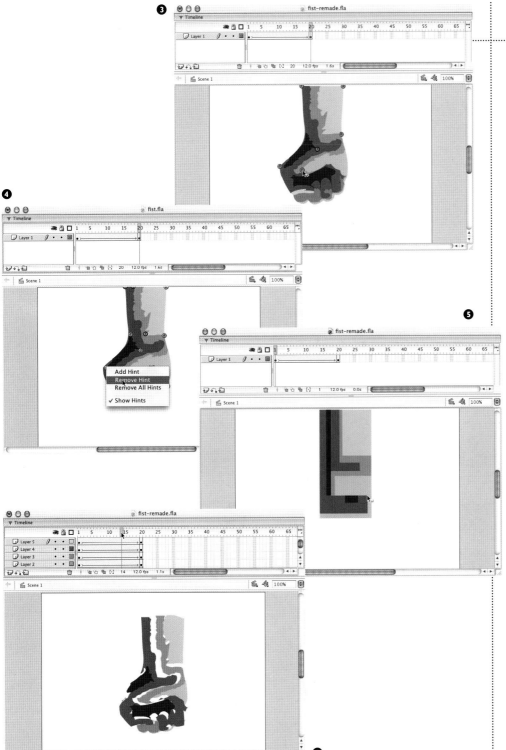

2 Go to *Shape* from the *Modify* menu and choose *Add Shape Hint*. A small circle with a letter will appear; drag this to a key point in the one graphic, then step to the other end of the tween and move the matching shape hint circle to the appropriate spot.

3 Add a few more, placing them carefully on the two shapes, then try the animation again. Sometimes shape hints can cause unexpected results, but in most cases they can tame unruly morphs.

4 If the hints start making the morph look worse, take a careful look at the beginning and ending images and move the hints around. If all else fails, try removing some; control-click or right-click on a hint, and choose *Remove Hint* from the contextual menu that appears. You'll find that fewer hints placed in strategic positions are more effective than half a dozen hints strewn around the place.

5 Remember, once a tween has been set up you can edit and even completely redraw out the original tween start and end points without having to remake the whole tween from scratch. It is a good idea to remove all hints first, and then remake those as necessary.

6 However, with complicated shapes, the best solution is often to use separate layers for different parts of the image. In this case, splitting the graphic up into layers according to color proved useful. This meant that just one or two shape hints were needed for each layer, and that some layers could be hidden while working on one set of shapes.

162 **PROJECT 32**
MATCHING FLASH MOVIE COLOR

Blending a Flash movie—or anything else, for that matter—into a Web page is easy if the page color is white or black; matching those extremes is simple. But because there is no way to make a Flash movie actually transparent on the page, you have to work a little to get things to blend seamlessly when the page background has a different hue. Blending Flash content into a page with a background image can be even more tricky, although there are ways to approach the problem. Just be aware that, in the flexible Web environment, getting the Flash movie aligned perfectly in a Web page with a complex background can be a hit-and-miss affair.

When setting the background color of a Flash movie, do make sure that you modify the background color itself. Drawing large, colored blocks in a layer can patch things up, but it can also cause slip-ups if you go back and develop the movie later. It is best to go to *Modify>Document*, then set the background color from there.

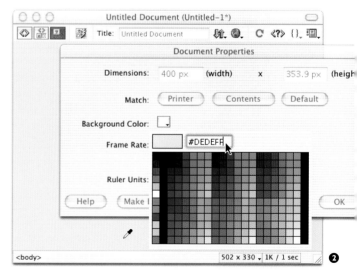

❸

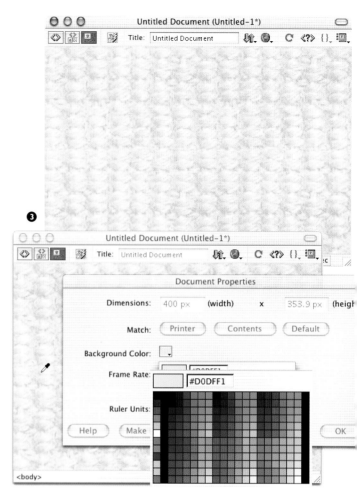

❷

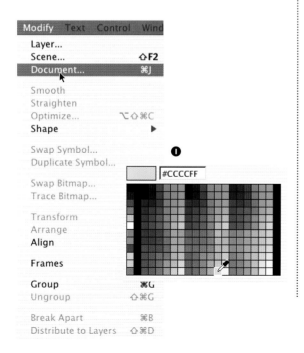

❶

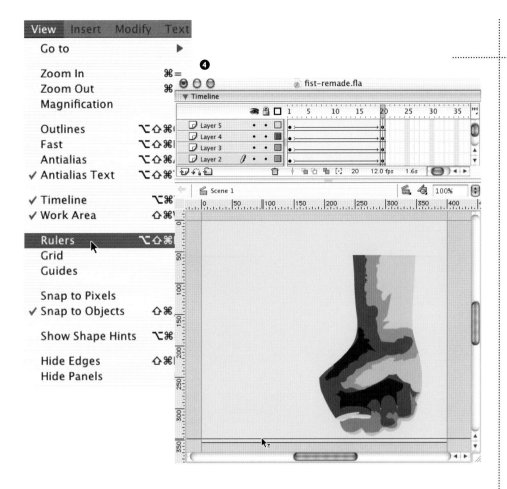

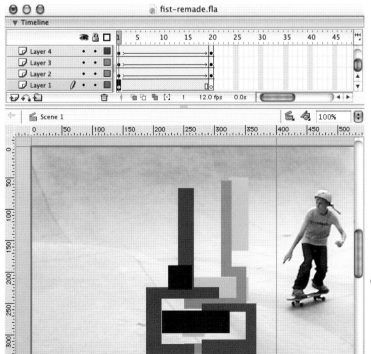

❶ If the destination Web page is filled with a Web-safe color then matching it in the Flash movie is a simple task. In Flash, go to the *Modify* menu and choose *Document*. Click the *Background Color* button to open the color picker panel, then click the color in the palette that matches your page.

❷ If you used a color that isn't Web-safe but you know the hexadecimal code, type it in the text field at the top of the pop-up color panel. If you are not sure of the exact color, just move the color sample tool away from the color panel and point at a visible part of your Web page. You may have to rearrange some windows in order to see things properly. You can't sample the color without clicking out of Flash, so make a note of the color code shown, then type it into Flash yourself.

❸ If the Web page is filled with a background image, you will have to decide how best to approach the problem. You can try to sample the most appropriate solid color for the Flash movie background, and in some cases that will give the right kind of results. However, you may want to try using a portion of the graphic within the Flash movie itself.

❹ First choose *Rulers* from the *View* menu, then drag out guides from the horizontal and vertical rulers to sit on the outsides of the movie area. Once you import images, you will find it hard to spot these edges, so this can help a lot.

❺ If the background image is a single large one, make a note of how far across and down in the page the Flash movie is to go. Then choose *Layer* from the *Insert* menu, choose *Import* from the *File* menu, and bring in the image.

164

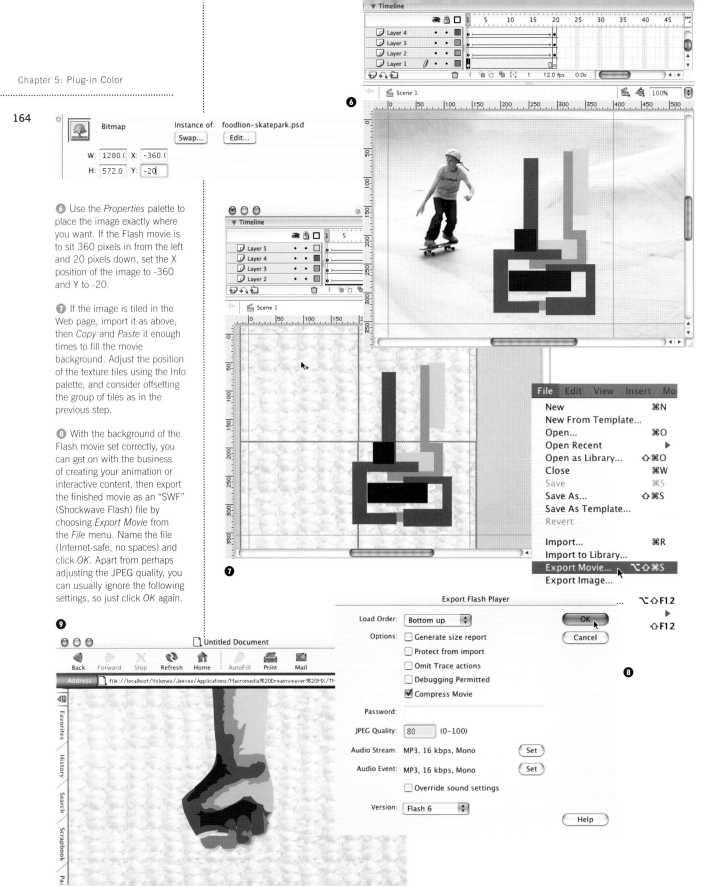

6 Use the *Properties* palette to place the image exactly where you want. If the Flash movie is to sit 360 pixels in from the left and 20 pixels down, set the X position of the image to -360 and Y to -20.

7 If the image is tiled in the Web page, import it as above, then *Copy* and *Paste* it enough times to fill the movie background. Adjust the position of the texture tiles using the Info palette, and consider offsetting the group of tiles as in the previous step.

8 With the background of the Flash movie set correctly, you can get on with the business of creating your animation or interactive content, then export the finished movie as an "SWF" (Shockwave Flash) file by choosing *Export Movie* from the *File* menu. Name the file (Internet-safe, no spaces) and click *OK*. Apart from perhaps adjusting the JPEG quality, you can usually ignore the following settings, so just click *OK* again.

❿

⓫

⓬

❾ Finally, bring your exported .swf file into your Web layout. In Dreamweaver, click the *Flash* icon in the *Insert* toolbar and choose the SWF file. In GoLive, drag the SWF object from the *Objects* palette into the page, then pick the SWF file using the *Inspector* palette. You will have to type the width and height of the movie manually, and there's no in-layout preview here either. In Freeway, draw out an HTML box and choose *Import* from the *File* menu, then fit and crop as necessary.

❿ **Dreamweaver** If you just need quick Flash buttons, Dreamweaver can make them itself, and you can pick the background color as well as pick a style and add your own text. Go to *Insert> Interactive Images> Flash Button*. Choose a button style, add and format your text, and finally select the appropriate background color from the pop-up palette.

⓫ **Freeway** If you use Freeway, you can control the background color of a Flash movie directly from the page layout. Go to the *Item* menu, then slide down to *Actions*, and pick *Flash Extras*. In the *Actions* palette (choose *Actions* in the *Window* menu if it isn't open), pick *Yes* from the *Edit Movie* pop-up, then select an option from the *Change BG Color* pop-up.

⓬ Pick *Item* and whatever color that has been assigned to the box itself will be applied to the movie. If you pick *Other*, a pop-up menu of standard colors (including an "Other" item for browsing more) is shown. The color change is not shown in the Freeway layout, but if you preview the page in a browser, you will see it has been applied.

166 **PROJECT 33**

TURNING COLOR BITMAPS INTO FLASH VECTORS

Flash is perfectly able to import a wide range of bitmap file formats into a movie. However, you should treat this ability carefully or you could end up with huge Flash files that keep people waiting online. If using bitmaps really is the only option, make sure that you are not importing high-resolution images into your Flash layouts, or you could inadvertently end up embedding much more image data than you need. Use Photoshop or Photoshop Elements to make sure that Image Size settings are 72 pixels per inch, and you should avoid this potential problem (but turn off *Resample Image* before changing the resolution numbers or you will lose image quality). Avoid scaling bitmap images up or down in Flash if you can, as Flash's scaling method is relatively crude. Even if you take care to avoid using high-resolution images, bitmaps will add bulk to your Flash movie.

There can be a better way to handle this: using Flash's ability to trace the image contours of a bitmap image and turn them into native drawn Flash shapes instead. Getting the settings for this right is the key, as it can easily deliver far too many parts for Flash to handle smoothly or—at the other extreme—hand you something ridiculously basic.

Ultimately you will have to decide whether using a regular bitmap or an autotraced replica is best for your needs. As with so much in Web design, you're dealing with a basic trade-off between quality and file size.

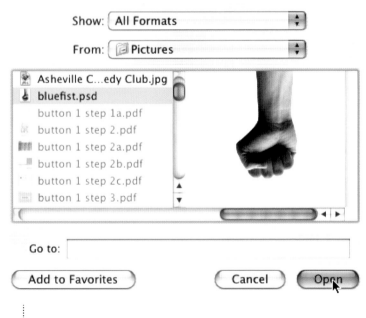

❷

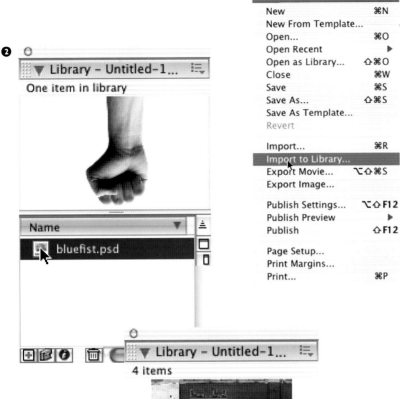

❸

❹

❶ Make a new document in Flash, then choose *File>Import* and select your image. The bitmap is imported onto the current layer and also placed into the document's library.

❷ To see the contents of this library, choose *Library* from the *Window* menu. If you use the imported image again in this movie—whether this is done by copying and pasting or by dragging it into place from the *Library* palette—it will be referenced from the library item, so your file does not get larger with each instance you add.

❸ You can import items to the library for use later without putting them into the movie itself. Choose *Import to Library* and select your image. It will appear in the *Library* palette, but not in your work area.

❹ To convert a bitmap image to an autotraced set of drawn shapes, select the graphic, then go to the *Modify* menu and choose *Trace Bitmap*. You will be asked to choose some conversion settings before Flash starts work.

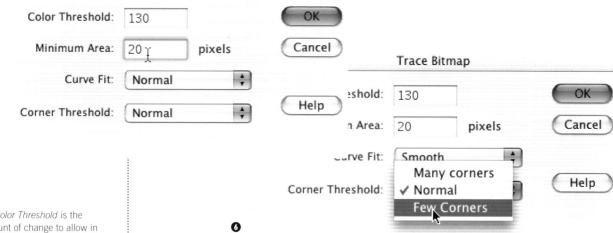

❺

❺ *Color Threshold* is the amount of change to allow in the image before Flash decides to start drawing new parts, while *Minimum Area* sets how large a bit of the image must be to be eligible for tracing.

❻ The two pop-up menus in this window also offer fine-tuning options. *Curve Fit* defines how faithful to the original the trace will try to be, while *Corner Threshold* specifies how readily Flash will generate corners in the shapes it produces. Setting them to tighter and more corners will usually make more realistic, but also more complex results. On the other hand, tracing strongly geometric images is best done with more corners allowed, even if the other settings are left at the simpler levels.

❼ Once a bitmap has been traced, the instance you were working with on the movie's canvas is replaced with the Flash graphic version. The original bitmap image is still available in the document's Library, so you can drag another instance of the graphic back onto the canvas if you want to make comparisons.

❻

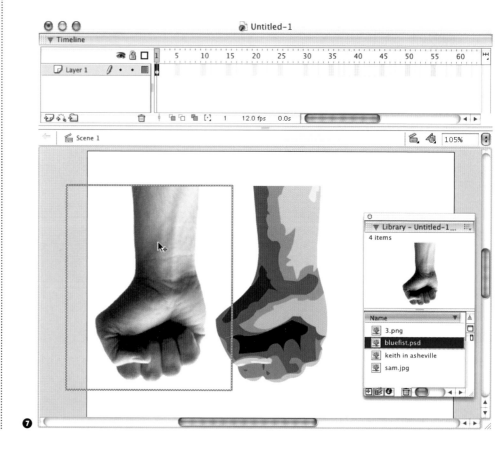

❼

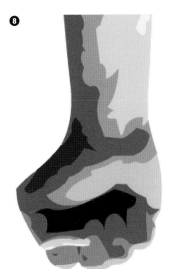
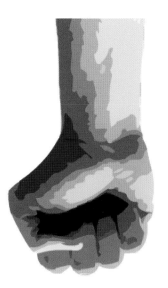
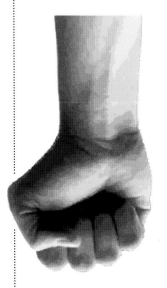

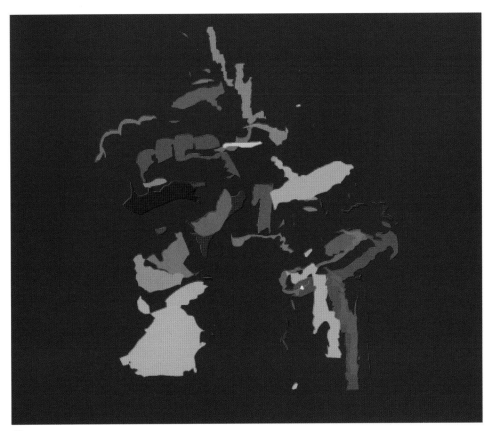

8 These three blue fists have been traced with different settings. The one on the left was traced with the *Threshold* set to 130, the *Minimum area* to 20, and *Curve fit* and *Corner set* to *Smooth* and *Few corners*. The middle was made with the default settings, and the right fist was traced with fairly strict settings and looks very much like the original image.

9 A traced image can be used for Flash specialties such as shape tweening. However, as there are usually many different elements in the traced result, the intermediate steps in a complex tween can look like scrap paper in a whirlwind. Even these "mistakes" can be turned into cool effects with shorter length tweens and on top of other elements, so don't be afraid to experiment!

170 PROJECT 34
USING QUICKTIME IN WEB PAGES

QuickTime is the multimedia standard established by Apple over ten years ago. It is the bedrock of the latest professional video editing suites, and also a very flexible way to deliver all sorts of video, animation, and audio content in Web pages.

For the serious QuickTime producer, it offers tricks such as multiple sound and text tracks (for captioning) and even video tracks to be embedded in a single movie, and then switched on and off according to different requirements. Multiple versions of a single movie can be held, with the appropriately sized one passed to the user depending on their connection speed. At the less technical end, it provides an interesting way to present video and other time-based data without having to deal with massive final file sizes.

Getting video into QuickTime format can be done on Macs and PCs with programs such as Adobe Premiere, but if you have a DV video camera, an Apple Mac, and Apple's free iMovie application, then this is the simplest way to get started with video editing and QuickTime production.

❶ Create your video using iMovie, Adobe Premiere, Windows Movie Maker or any other video-editing package, and export it as a QuickTime movie. If you have the option, consider the color in your movie and try to tune it to suit your overall site design.

❷ Use whatever export options your package has to keep the file size down to a managable extent. Small dimensions (under 320 x 240 pixels), fewer frames per second (12 or under), and heavy audio compression (if applicable) are all options that are worth considering.

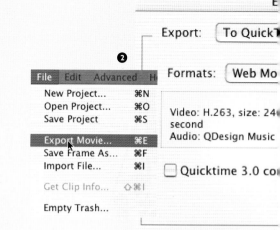

3 Dreamweaver Once the QuickTime movie is prepared, you can place it in a Web page. In Dreamweaver go to the *Insert* menu, and slide down to *Media*, and choose *Plug-in*. Dreamweaver shows only a placeholder item, but you can use the *Play* button in the *Properties* palette to preview the movie on the page.

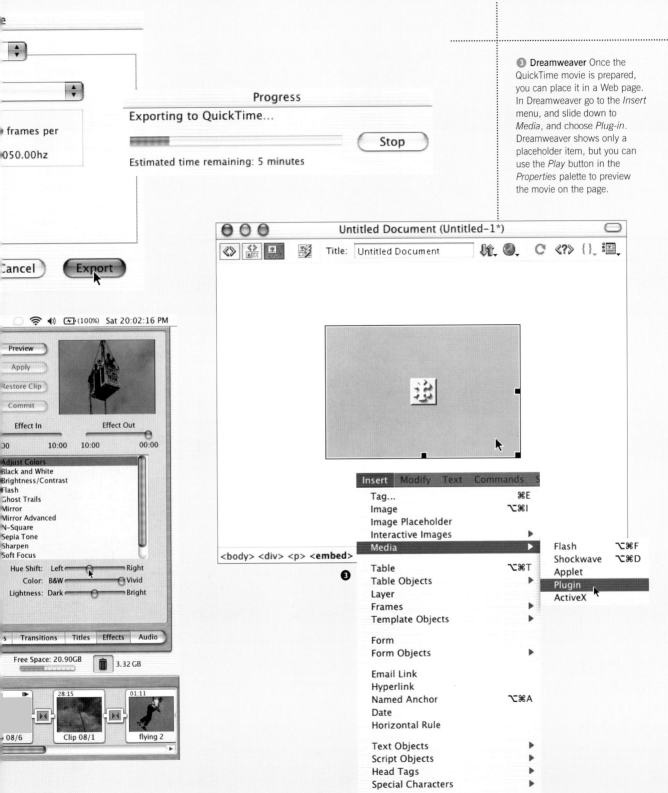

❹ You can use the *Properties* palette to adjust the pixel dimensions of the movie. Unfortunately there isn't much more offered for fine-tuning the behavior of the movie in the Web page, and the code made as standard isn't particularly up-to-date and trips up some of the latest Windows browsers.

❺ **GoLive** GoLive has better support for media such as QuickTime. Set up a new GoLive document, then drag a QuickTime object from the *Objects* palette into the page. In the *Inspector* palette, click the folder button and pick the movie. The QuickTime object is automatically scaled to the size of the movie, and the most broadly compatible HTML coding method is applied..

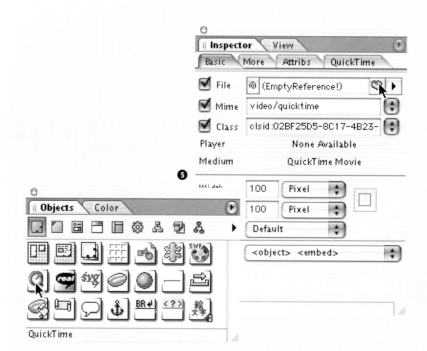

 **6**

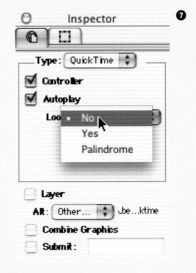 **7**

6 **Freeway** Freeway's QuickTime support is also good. In a Freeway layout, draw out an HTML box and choose *Import* from the *File* menu. Pick the movie, then go to *Graphic* in the *Item* menu and choose *Fit Box to Graphic*.

7 In the *Inspector* palette are settings for autoplaying the movie, showing or hiding the playback controller, and looping options. Like GoLive, the code Freeway generates is complete and compatible with all the latest Web browsers.

8 If the QuickTime movie's controller was set to be hidden, the user will see nothing but the movie itself in the Web page. This option makes it harder (although by no means impossible) for someone to save the movie to their computer. If the movie is set to autoplay, it will begin playing as soon as a sizable buffer segment has been downloaded by the browser. If autoplay is off and the controller is hidden, the user can start playback by double-clicking the movie, although you should include some element that tells them to do so on the finished page.

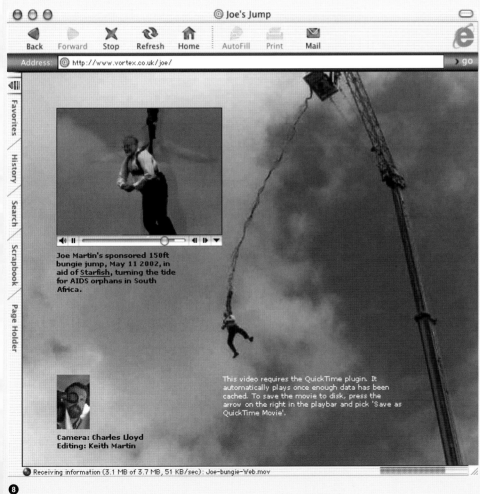

8

174 PROJECT 35
USING QUICKTIME VR IN WEB PAGES

One of the most magical non-video uses of QuickTime is the QuickTime VR movie format. A VR movie is a still image, but one built from a series of pictures that make up a partial or complete photographic "sweep" of a scene. The result is an image that can be panned around in all directions, enabling the viewer to look around the scene.

Done the normal way, a set of photos (preferably wideangle and taken with a tripod) are "stitched" together to create a single panoramic image. Then that file is embedded and shown in the VR movie, with a measure of distortion correction applied to make it feel realistic.

The stitched panoramic image can be touched up in Photoshop before being converted to the final VR movie, and this is where photo manipulation and coloring tricks can really be effective. Airbrushing the top and bottom of the image to match the page background can blend the VR movie into the rest of the page in an almost spooky manner.

And of course, with the right subject matter, you can add all sorts of graphic extras to your panoramic image. You can even make one from scratch and import that as the source for a VR movie, producing a navigable illustration of a scene or a full-blown abstract visual experiment. A VR movie can also include clickable "hot spots" that link to other movies and even different Web pages.

There are a few programs available that produce QuickTime VR movies, but one of the most sophisticated is The VR Worx, from VR Toolbox. Demo versions are available for the Mac (including Mac OS X) and for Windows if you want to try it out.

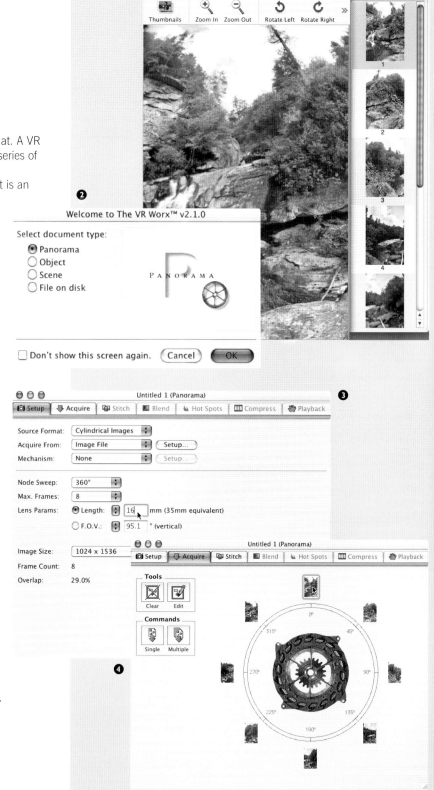

❶ When taking the photos for a panorama, try to use a wideangle lens and a tripod, and turn off automatic light metering. You can use a handheld camera, but the shots will demand more work during the final assembly.

❷ Launch The VR Worx and pick *Panorama* as the document type, to create a panoramic view made from several images, stitched together.

❸ First, put in the details of the images. This particular project uses a 360° set of photos, taken with a regular 35mm film camera with a 16mm lens. There are only eight shots taken (the bare minimum) and each image is 1,024 x 1,536 pixels, taken straight from a Photo CD.

❹ Next, click the *Acquire* tab. Import the images, making sure they are in the right order. Note that images can be rotated by 90° or 180° as they are imported, if necessary.

❺ Click the *Stitch* tab, then the *Stitch* button near the top of the window. After some processing, The VR Worx will present the photos, warped to roughly the correct positions. If needed, you can adjust the results manually.

❻ After you have nudged the images as much as you think is necessary, click the *Blend* tab, then the *Blend* button. Once this is done, choose *Export* from the *File* menu. Save the image to disk, then open it up again in Photoshop or another image-editing application.

❼ Retouch the image, checking carefully for examples of ghosted double-imaging. Do what you can using the various touch up tools, then save as a non-layered image and quit.

⑫

⑬

❽ Back in The VR Worx, go back to the *Setup* tab, and pick *Single Panorama* from the *Source Format* pop-up menu. Click *OK* when asked about discarding the work you have done so far. Select *Acquire*, then *Import* the edited image.

❾ Go straight to the *Compress* tab. The default compression method, Photo JPEG, is okay, but the quality level should be dropped to the minimum to make a final file small enough for Web use. Try out other compressors as well—Sorenson 3 is very efficient, but tends to make images look a little like paintings. Switch to the *Playback* tab and check the file size in the bottom-right.

❿ You can change the size and the width-to-height ratio of the final movie by just scaling it here. You can also choose which viewpoint will be the one shown when the movie first loads, and how far in and out the viewer can zoom. When you are happy, click *Export Movie*.

⓫ Place the QuickTime VR movie into a Web page just as you would a regular QuickTime movie. The VR controller shows the zoom buttons, but users can also zoom by pressing the Shift or Control keys.

⑫ Such dynamic graphics don't always blend well into a page, but at times it's more effective to make these items stand out. Here, a PNG format transparent shadow graphic (a black square blurred in Fireworks) has been placed behind the movie.

⑬ The result is a set of sliced images that surround the movie on the page. Everything on the page has a muted tone, which makes the movie's saturated color stand out even more.

PROJECT 36

BLENDING MOVIES AND BACKGROUND COLORS

When a video clip is placed on a page, most people expect it to be a simple rectangular image—something added to a layout rather than camouflaged in any way. But, although a movie does have to be shown within a rectangular shape, it doesn't have to look like that. By using video masks and layers in the movie you can come up with videos which look anything but ordinary, and fit into all sorts of Web page designs with ease.

First of all, to work through this project and the one that follows, you will need to have the "Pro" version of QuickTime installed on your Mac or PC. This is the enhanced form of the free QuickTime Player available from the Apple website. It costs $30 (or comes free with many commercial QuickTime editing programs), and enables all sorts of editing tricks in the apparently innocuous QuickTime Player application.

❷

❶

❸

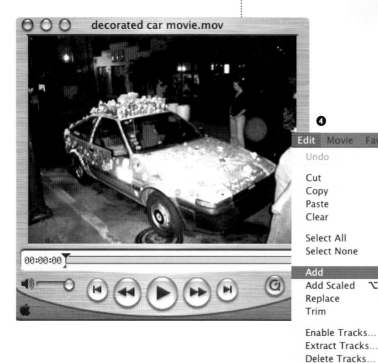

❹

1 First, the basics. Copying and pasting movies together is simple. Picking *Select All* and then *Copy* from the *Edit* menu, puts the movie on the clipboard, ready for pasting. When pasted (again via the *Edit* menu), it is inserted wherever the playback head happens to be in the current movie.

2 To select just a portion of a movie rather than the whole thing, move the playback head (the black arrow at the top of the timeline) to one end of the segment, then hold down the Shift key and click or drag to the other end. This selects that chunk of the movie, shown in gray in the timeline bar, with markers at either end. Drag either marker to fine-tune the selection before copying.

3 Rather than just pasting segments of movies together in sequence, you can layer them on top of each other. Handling and synchronizing multiple layers of time-based media is one of QuickTime's strengths. To see what layers a movie has, choose *Get Movie Properties* from the *Movie* menu, then look in the first pop-up menu in the *Properties* window. Most movies will have either a single video track, or one video and one sound track. (Using the *Enable Tracks*, *Extract Tracks* and *Delete Tracks* options in the *Edit* menu can help manage things).

4 Open a second movie and select the whole thing, then go back to the first movie. Move the playback head to the beginning, then go to the *Edit* menu. The important options here are *Add* and *Add Scaled*, although *Replace* and *Trim* can be useful at times. Choosing *Add* places the copied movie clip into the current movie as a new layer.

5 The new track is likely to be a different size both in dimensions and in time. To adjust the dimensions, pick the new video track in the *Properties* menu (it will be the bottom-most one), then choose *Size* from the second pop-up menu. Click the *Adjust* button, and resize the movie as necessary, then click *Done* when finished. Even if the size is the same, this can be useful for scaling down to make an inset movie or rotate the track.

6 To fix the problem of one of the clips being too long, you can just select the extra portion in the timeline and choose *Clear* from the *Edit* menu. Or, to stretch or squash a clip to fit the length of the currently selected portion of video when pasted, choose *Add Scaled* instead of *Add*. This option is particularly useful for adding a static graphic as a video layer to the whole length of a movie.

7 Now we will use these layering features to make an irregular mask shape for our movie. First, prepare a mask graphic in a graphics program such as Photoshop. In an image the size of your movie, make a black shape. This will be the apparent visible boundary of the movie. Save it to disk; GIF, TIFF, PICT, or JPEG formats are fine.

180

8 Now open up your movie. (First close without saving changes if you still have the previous steps visible). For this example, we will add a simple static decorative graphic as a video track. *Copy* a suitably sized graphic from a program such as Photoshop. It can be a flat color (to match a flat Web page fill color) or it can be something more complex. Step back to the movie and choose *Select All* from the *Edit* menu, then choose *Add Scaled*.

9 The graphic is stretched to fit the movie's length, and covers the video completely. Now open the *Properties* window and pick *Video Track 2* from the first pop-up menu, then *Mask* from the second. Click *Set*, and choose your black and white mask image. The black and white areas hide and show parts of the track they're masking. Click *Invert* if the wrong parts are hidden.

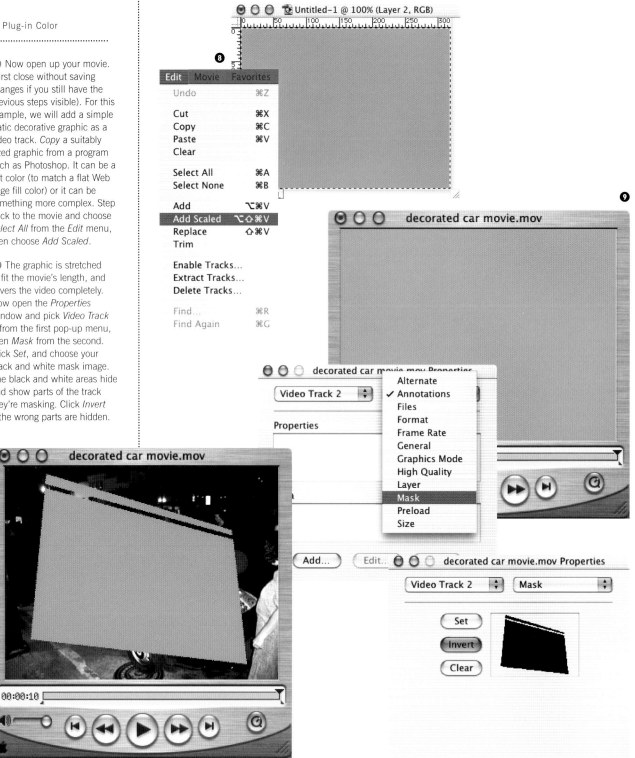

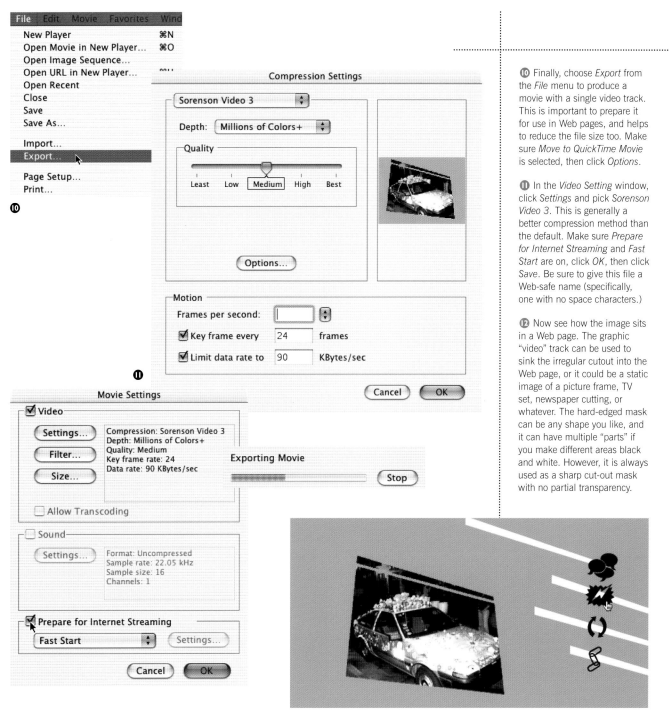

❿ Finally, choose *Export* from the *File* menu to produce a movie with a single video track. This is important to prepare it for use in Web pages, and helps to reduce the file size too. Make sure *Move to QuickTime Movie* is selected, then click *Options*.

⓫ In the *Video Setting* window, click *Settings* and pick *Sorenson Video 3*. This is generally a better compression method than the default. Make sure *Prepare for Internet Streaming* and *Fast Start* are on, click *OK*, then click *Save*. Be sure to give this file a Web-safe name (specifically, one with no space characters.)

⓬ Now see how the image sits in a Web page. The graphic "video" track can be used to sink the irregular cutout into the Web page, or it could be a static image of a picture frame, TV set, newspaper cutting, or whatever. The hard-edged mask can be any shape you like, and it can have multiple "parts" if you make different areas black and white. However, it is always used as a sharp cut-out mask with no partial transparency.

182 PROJECT 37
BLENDING MOVIES AND BACKGROUND COLORS 2

Making a movie show within a sharp-edged mask can be a highly effective way to present video content in a Web page—or any other presentation medium for that matter. But you are not restricted to just such high-contrast clipped edges. There is actually a way to use a soft-edged mask in QuickTime movies, enabling you to mix layers together in a much more convincing manner. This process uses the transparency abilities of the PNG file format to create a graphic "video" layer with 8-bit transparency—a full 256 different strengths of opacity from solid through to clear. The final result does not demand a high-end system to view, and even producing the content doesn't take anything more than a standard graphics program and the QuickTime Pro Player.

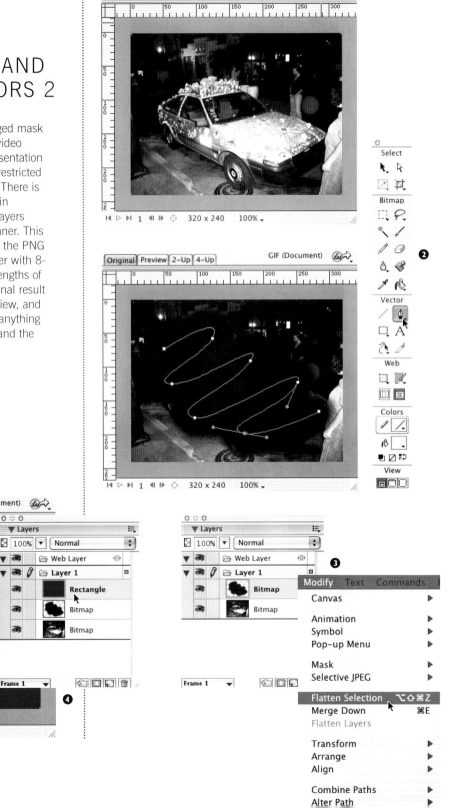

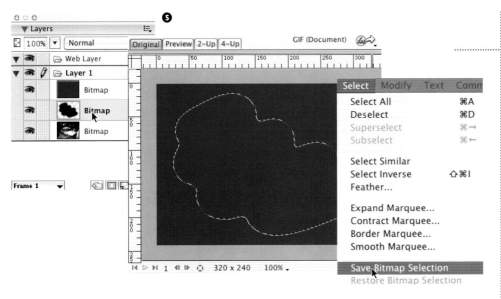

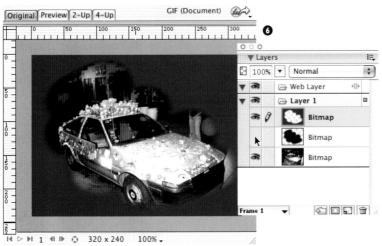

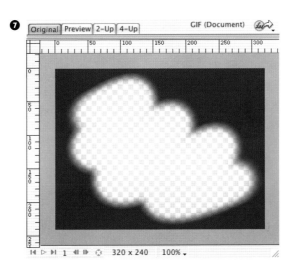

❶ First, prepare the mask using Photoshop, Photoshop Elements, or Fireworks. *Copy* a frame from the movie, then *Paste* it into a new document in your image editing program—in this case, Fireworks. This will be a useful guide.

❷ The mask for this movie is made initially with the *Pen* tool, faking a soft sprayed shape. The path was drawn, then the stroke was set to 60 pixels and the edge softness set to 100, using the *Properties* palette.

❸ Once drawn, the path must be converted to a bitmap by choosing *Flatten Selection* from the *Modify* menu. This turns the path layer into a bitmap image of the shape just drawn.

❹ Now make a new layer and fill it with the static image that will surround the movie. This can be designed to merge with the rest of the page, or to be a decorative surround. If you use a rectangle with custom fills, convert it to a bitmap—select the layer, then choose *Modify> Flatten Selection*.

❺ In the *Layers* palette, command-click (Mac users) or control-click (Windows users) the layer with the mask shape to make a selection from that layer's image data. Click the layer with your new image.

❻ Press the Delete key on the keyboard to *Cut* the selection from your image. Hide the shape layer and show the layer with the movie frame to make sure it looks as you expect. If it does, delete that layer.

❼ You should now be able to see the checkerboard transparency pattern through the cut-out portion of the image. If not, go to *Modify>Canvas> Canvas Color*, and click the *Transparent* option.

184

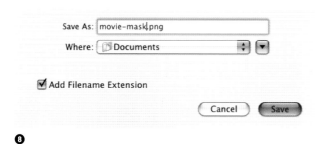

❽

❾

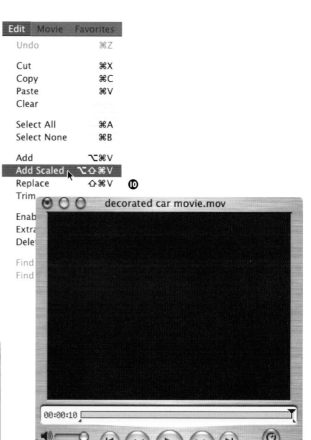

❿

⓫

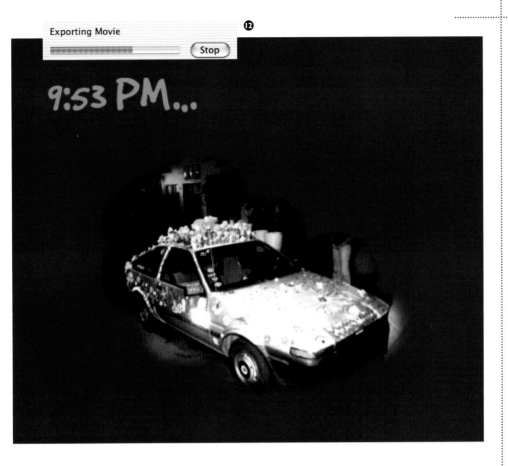

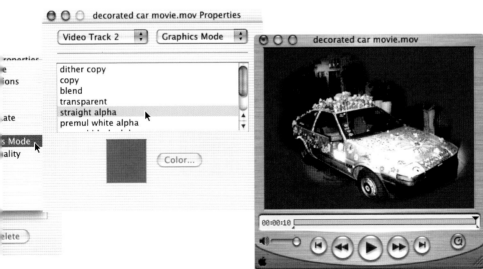

8 Save this image as a PNG file. In Fireworks, this is the regular file format, but in Photoshop you will need to pick this format manually.

9 Go back to the QuickTime Player and choose *Import* from the *File* menu. Pick the file you just made, and it will be converted to a short movie. No transparency will be visible yet.

10 Choose *Select All*, then *Copy* from the *Edit* menu, and finally go to your movie and choose *Add Scaled* from the *Edit* menu. This adds it to the movie as a new track, running the full length of the original video clip. However, it completely hides the actual movie track.

11 Choose *Get Movie Properties* from the *Movie* menu, and pick the new video track from the first pop-up menu, then pick *Graphics Mode* from the second. A number of different modes are offered, but the one needed here is *Straight Alpha*. This uses the transparency information to hide parts of the graphic track, showing the next track down as a result.

12 Export the movie following steps 10 and 11 from project 36, then place it into your Web page layout. If you hide the controller and set autoplay to true, the effect can be quite startling as the image, apparently painted onto the page, comes to life.

Reference

Glossary

active hyperlink The currently selected link in a web browser, often differentiated from other links that appear on the same page by being displayed in another color.

additive colors The color model describing the primary colors of transmitted light: red, green, and blue (RGB). Additive colors can be mixed to form all other colors in photographic reproduction and computer display monitors.

aliasing The term describing the jagged appearance of bitmapped images or fonts, either when the resolution is insufficient or when they have been enlarged.

artifact A visible flaw in an electronically prepared image, usually occurring as a result of compression or an imaging technique employed.

banding An aberration that occurs in the electronic reproduction of graduated tints, when the ratio of halftone screen ruling and output resolution is incorrect, causing a "stepped" appearance.

bit A contraction of binary digit, the smallest piece of information a computer can use. A bit is expressed as one of two values, which can be a 1 or 0.

bit depth The number of bits assigned to each pixel in a digital image. One-bit will only produce black and white (the bit is either on or off), 8-bit will generate 256 grays or colors, while 24-bit will produce 16.7 million colors. Also called color depth.

bitmap graphic An image made up of dots or pixels, and usually generated by paint or image-editing applications, as distinct from the vector images drawing applications.

blend The merging of two or more colors, forming a gradual transition from one to the other.

calibration The process of adjusting a machine or piece of hardware to conform to a known scale or standard so that it performs more accurately.

chroma The intensity, or purity, of a color, and thus its degree of saturation.

CMYK abbr.: Cyan, Magenta, Yellow, BlacK. The four printing-process colors based on the subtractive color model (black is represented by K, which stands for key plate).

color correction The process of adjusting color values in reproduction in order to achieve a desired result.

color model The method of defining or modifying color. Although there are many proprietary color models, such as PANTONE®, FOCOLTONE, TRUMATCH, TOYO, and DIC, the two generic models are those based on the way light is transmitted—the "additive" and "subtractive" color models.

color picker A color model displayed on a computer monitor. Color pickers may be specific to an application (Adobe Photoshop), a third-party color model (PANTONE®), or to the operating system running on your computer.

color temperature A measure of the composition of light. This is defined as the temperature—measured in degrees Kelvin—to which a black object would need to be heated to produce a particular color of light.

complementary colors Two colors that sit directly opposite each other on the color wheel. Combined they theoretically form white or black, depending on the color model.

compression The technique of rearranging data so that it either occupies less space on disk or transfers faster between devices or on communication lines.

contrast The degree of difference between adjacent tones in an image, from the lightest to the darkest. High contrast describes an image with light highlights and dark shadows but with few shades in between, whereas a low-contrast image has even tones and few dark areas or highlights.

CSS abbr.: Cascading Style Sheets. A language defined by a World Wide Web Consortium recommendation for specifying the appearance (fonts, positioning, color, etc.) of the elements of an HTML document.

definition The overall quality—or clarity—of an image, determined by the combined subjective effect of grain (or resolution in a digital image) and sharpness.

dithering A term used to refer to the use of patterns of pixels of available colors, for example, the colors in a Web "safe" palette, to simulate missing colors, based upon the principle of optical mixing.

frame On the Web, a means of displaying more than one page at a time within a single window. The window is divided into separate areas (frames), each one displaying a separate page.

gamma A measure of contrast in a digital image, a photographic film or paper, or processing technique.

HSL hue, saturation, lightness) A color model based upon the light transmitted either in an image or in your monitor—hue being the spectral color, saturation being the intensity of the color pigment, and lightness representing the strength of luminance from light to dark.

HTML abbr.: Hypertext Markup Language. A text-based language used to format documents published on the World Wide Web, and which can be viewed with a Web browser.

hue Pure spectral color, which distinguishes a color from others. Red is a different hue from blue; and although light red and dark red may contain varying amounts of white or black, they may be the same hue.

ICC (International Color Consortium) Organization responsible for defining cross-application color standards.

image slicing The practice of dividing up a digital image into rectangular areas or slices, which can then be optimized or animated independently.

keyframe In traditional animation the key drawings or "extremes" show the position of characters, etc. at the start and finish of a movement or action. These key drawings are done first, and then the in-between drawings (tweens) are created to complete the illusion of a smooth or effective movement. Keyframes are the digital equivalent

lightness The tonal measure of a color relative to a scale running from black and white. Also called "brightness" or "value" in certain color systems.

mouseover The mouse event that occurs when the mouse pointer rolls over a navigation button.

PANTONE® The registered trademark of Pantone Inc.'s system of color standards and control and quality requirements, in which each color bears a description of its formulation (in percentages) for subsequent printing.

pastel shades Shades of color that are generally both lighter and less saturated than their equivalent bright hue.

pixel abbr.: picture element. The smallest component of any digitally generated image, including text, such as a single dot of light on a computer screen.

plug-in Software, usually developed by a third party, which extends the capabilities of another application. Plug-ins are used to add video and audio support to browsers.

resolution The degree of quality, definition, or clarity with which an image is reproduced or displayed, for example, in a photograph, or via a scanner, monitor, printer, or other output device.

RGB abbr.: Red, Green, Blue. The primary colors of the "additive" color model which applies to onscreen use.

saturation The variation in color of the same tonal brightness from none (gray), through pastel shades (low saturation), to pure color with no gray (high saturation, or "fully saturated"). Also called "purity" or "chroma."

sharpening Enhancing the apparent sharpness of an image by increasing the contrast between adjacent pixels.

subtractive colors The color model describing the primary colors of reflected light: cyan, magenta, and yellow (CMY). Subtractive colors form the basis for printed process colors.

tag The formal name for a formatting command in a markup language, as in the case of HTML.

tint The shade created when white is added to a solid color.

tween A contraction of "in-between." An animator's term for the process of creating the transitional frames that fit in between the keyframes in an animation.

vector graphic Images made up of mathematically defined shapes, lines, curves and fills, which can be displayed at any size or resolution without loss of quality.

Index

Useful Websites

Download resources
www.versiontracker.com
www.downloads.com
www.fonts.com
www.acidfonts.com
www.thepluginsite.com
www.flashkit.com
www.softpress.com/actions
www.freewayactions.com
www.vischeck.com
www.vrtollbox.com
www.easypano.com

Web design and creative information
www.wpdfd.com
www.biggles.uk.com
www.vortex.co.uk
www,macuser.co.uk

Examples
www.fray.com
www.bigbridgesolutions.com
www.the5k.org
www.shockwave.com

Software
www.adobe.com
www.macromedia.com
www.microsoft.com
www.apple.com
www.ulead.com
www.corel.com
www.softpress.com
www.netscape.com
www.jasc.com

Tutorials
www.adobe.com/products/tips/golive.html
www.adobe.com/products/tips/photoshop.html
www.webmonkey.com
www.computerarts.co.uk
www.createonline.co.uk
www.creativepro.com
www.maccentral.com
www.creativebase.com
www.planetphotoshop.com
www.softpress.com/askanna
www.softpress.com/tutorials

Acknowledgments

With thanks to my mother, Linette Martin, who showed me how to write and how to enjoy language, to Nell Harden, for teaching me the disciplines of language structure, and to Biggles, for ongoing creative inspirations, encouragement and fun..